McGruber's
Folly

Max Braithwaite

McCLELLAND AND STEWART

The Canadian Publishers
McClelland and Stewart Limited
25 Hollinger Road, Toronto M4B 3G2

CANADIAN CATALOGUING IN PUBLICATION DATA

Braithwaite, Max, 1911-
  McGruber's folly

ISBN 0-7710-1613-1

I. Title.

PS8503.R34M33   C813'.54   C81-094087-6
PR9199.3.B73M33

This is a work of fiction. Any resemblance
to persons living or dead is purely coincidental.

Printed in the United States of America

CHAPTER ONE

Ranse McGruber could never remember afterwards exactly when he got the crazy idea. It may have been when he was watching the Lotto Canada show and comparing the numbers on his ticket with the ones printed on the television screen. Or it may have been when he was walking down the Shorebank Road towards the river with his binoculars dangling from his hard, wrinkled neck and the deer flies trying to get through his beard. Or maybe it was when he was out in the canoe fishing bass off Blueberry Point.

When he first got the idea, he thought of it as a great plot for a play. Ranse was always doing that. Even when he was a young cop on the beat in Toronto, walking up Jarvis Street with a partner (you never went on Jarvis Street alone in those days) he got ideas for stories. Later, when he was a detective and still later as a chief of detectives, he was convinced that since a policeman runs into so many weird situations he was a natural to become a writer of mystery plays. But he never did write anything.

He didn't have the time. His job kept him busy during the day and often at night, too. And when he did have time off, he liked to spend it with his family. No boys, but two girls can take up a lot of a father's time.

Then there were the long, happy hours he'd put in as a member of the Scarborough Dramatic Club, play-acting, pretending to be somebody else. He'd loved it. Sometimes the others (mostly women) would express amazement at a cop who was interested in Little Theatre. There was one young socialite, whom he remembered fondly, who let her interest become very personal indeed. He'd had plenty of roles–there was always a shortage of men in theatre groups–and one director had even suggested that he should take up the career seriously. But with a family to support the risk had been too great. He remembered particularly his role as the killer in *Night Must Fall*. It proved, once again, that no one ever knew what lay beneath the exterior of a man.

A family to support. He thought of Helen and Susie. He'd always wanted a boy, but nobody could have asked for two finer girls. But now, in no time at all it seemed, they were gone. Helen, the youngest, off to Regina, so far away that he seldom saw her. And Susie, living in Toronto and, like her mother, married to a cop. He chuckled to himself when he thought of her twin boys, Timmy and Patrick. What a pair.

How those kids liked to fish! Good at it, too. He'd never been able to get his girls to go fishing with him. Said it was yucky. But Tim and Pat couldn't get enough of it. They only came once in a while, on weekends and in the summer holidays. Not for the whole two months or anything like that. Their father, Zeke, wanted them to go to scout camp. He'd never been able to go to camp as a kid because his folks never had enough money, and he'd always hoped that his kids would go. But the twins hated the idea, preferring to be at Wigwam Lake fishing with their grandfather. Ranse preferred that, too.

When the kids weren't there, life was pretty boring. It was the boredom as much as the greed that helped promote the plan. Josie fit right into the community. She had her own Datsun and would drive into Port Perkins to her bridge club and her quilting club and her gardening club. One winter, she'd even driven the fifteen miles to Deepford to take pottery lessons at night school. Well, she sure had the skill for it. But him, he didn't do any of those things. Hated bridge. Tried the local little theatre, but the old magic was gone. So, he did a little partridge hunting in the fall, fooled around with his gun collection, fished, of course, and now and then drank with the guys at the Legion Hall.

Come to think of it, it may have been a chance remark by Tip Tipton when they were playing four-handed crib at the Legion that first planted the seed that grew into the great idea. The guys were kidding him about his beard, as they did when there was nothing else to do, and Tip remarked that he'd never seen Ranse without the beard. "Wouldn't know you if I met you on the street without all that brush covering your phisog. What do you really look like anyway?"

"You'll never find out," Ranse had told him.

"Probably homelier 'n a hedge fence," somebody else commented, and then added, "for crumb's sake, Tip, it's your play."

Ranse hadn't thought anything of it at the time, but maybe it had been working away in his subconscious mind. Ranse was something of a student of the subconscious. As a detective, he'd taken the requisite course in criminal psychology and, after the course was finished, had got more books on the subject.

Everybody stole something. Whether it was kids pinching hubcaps or salesmen padding expense accounts or company presidents stealing from their own firms to cheat the income-tax people. And the motive was always the same, he'd concluded. Greed. The desire to get their hands on more money, a lot more money than they could ever possibly save or earn. Plain ordinary greed. One of the seven deadly sins. Well, covetousness, really, but greed was the same.

But these were Catholic sins and Ranse wasn't a Catholic.

Come to that, he wasn't anything. Forty years as a cop sort of takes it out of you. You see too much of the seamy side of life, of the people who have never had a chance. Born in poverty, learning almost from their mothers' knees that they'd never have a chance for the good life. There was no justice. But Ranse had never been in-

9

terested in justice; his concern was with the law. His job was to arrest law-breakers and turn them over to the court. What happened to them after that was somebody else's business.

As he must have told a thousand people in his day, "I don't make the laws; I just try to enforce them."

As a matter of fact, he considered most of the laws to be nuts. But you didn't think of them: that was the only way to function. When you busted a long-haired teenager for having a few reefers in his jeans, you couldn't let yourself think of the doctors and lawyers and, yes, cops who smoked regularly. The real, the only, crime was in getting caught.

Ranse McGruber determined that he would never get caught.

The thing was that crimes were committed by criminals. So each time a robbery was committed, the cops checked on the whereabouts of the known criminals, the potential criminals, and the informers who lived with and knew the criminals. There was always something to point to them. But what if an honest man committed a robbery? What then?

The threat of poverty gnawed at Ranse's brain as a wolf gnaws at a caribou leg. When he was young and storing up plots in his fertile mind, he always considered that it would be writing that would lift him out of his situation. He'd read about Arthur Hailey, the editorial drudge who turned millionaire by writing television plays and then novels that sold in the millions, and who lived in the Bahamas. And John D. MacDonald, who turned out crime stories by the dozen and fished for marlin off the Florida coast instead of for paltry little bass in Wigwam Lake.

He longed to fish for marlin, Ranse did. To get into his fishing launch, which he would name the *Pilar*, after Hemingway's boat, and go out into the Gulf Stream and fight the big ones. But no girls. He'd take Josie with him. After all, like him she suffered through the long years of penury and deserved better things. It made him feel virtuous and good to think of taking Josie with him.

But it hadn't worked out. When he finally reached the point where he had the time and the solitude so necessary to a writer, he didn't have the energy. And the great plots that had been kicking around in his mind all these years just didn't work when he tried to commit them to paper.

But, oh Lord, how he tried. He bought a typewriter and built an addition onto the cottage for an office. It took him all that first summer to complete the office. Getting the cement blocks and then digging down to bedrock, all took time. Laying the blocks, getting them straight, that was the really hard part. He had plenty of help from his neighbours, but most of it was advice and helping him take beer breaks. The carpentry work and the insulation went faster. He put in an immense picture window that gave him a great view of the lake and the motorboats and water-skiers who inhabited it on weekends. The view was good, but the noise was loud.

He'd scrounged around at barn sales and got a desk and a chair and a bookcase and an old wooden file cabinet and he was ready to go. But there'd been nowhere to go. He'd sat in front of the typewriter for hours and nothing would come; then he'd looked out the window at the boats and mentally computed the cost of each big power boat that went by. That one must have cost five thousand and that one more like seven and so on. He would have much bigger boats when his play was produced.

Or he'd think of being interviewed on television talk shows:

"When did you first get the idea to write this play, Mr. McGruber?"

"Oh it's been kicking around in my head for some time. I thought it would never come out."

"Well, it did, and we're all very glad that it did, and that it has become such a huge success. Tell me, have you had any movie offers?"

"Yes, a couple, but nothing I can talk about definitely."

"It will make a wonderful movie."

"Thank you."

"No, thank you. My guest has been . . . ."

But when he'd turned back to the typewriter, to compose the scenes and acts and dialogue that would add up to a big hit, nothing would come. He drank gallons of coffee, sharpened dozens of pencils, and even persuaded a doctor he knew in Toronto to prescribe some amphetamines for him. They revved him up, all right, and made him a little dizzy, but didn't produce any great writing.

He'd devised other projects to keep him out of the office–building a boathouse, then a dock, then a new pumphouse. When winter had come, he'd spent more and more time drinking beer at the Legion, playing cards and darts, and beguiling his friends with the stories he should have been committing to paper.

He even tried a course in creative writing at the high school in Deepford. "Discover those hidden talents in yourself. Remember Grandma Moses." But what the instructor, a moonlighting high-school English teacher, tried to teach had nothing to do with the kinds of scripts he wanted to write. Good fiction, he knew, didn't depend on proper grammar and paragraph structure. That was just for academics.

It was no use. He would never make his fortune writing.

There was another and easier way–Lotto Canada. One million dollars first prize! Given away regularly. He bought as many five-dollar tickets as he could afford and in as many different locations as he could reach. Altogether, he had ten tickets at five dollars each. Fifty dollars was a lot of money.

On the night of the draw, he and Josie watched the show, so excited they couldn't sit still. It was a monster television production called "Cash For Life," with a slick host in a white suit and fuzzy hair, and seven celebrities, each of whom spun a big wheel with numbers on it. Where the pointer stopped, that was the number. But first there were songs and interviews. A black girl in a red, white and blue muumuu sang "You might as well be rich/Health is fine but you can't beat wealth/So everybody come! And join the Lotto fun!"

One of the wheel-spinners told a story about how Lotto Canada was helping to fund their Recreation for Seniors project.

"To hell with that," Ranse had stormed. "Let's win some real money!"

Ranse and Josie each had five tickets spread on the TV trays in front of them, ready to check against those on the screen. The first celebrity spun his wheel. It stopped at two, bending the pointer as it tried to go to three. Ranse let out a whoop as he saw that one of his tickets began with a two.

"We're away now! Let her go for number seven!"

But they didn't let her go. Instead, they brought in a skinny youth who was riding his bicycle across the country from North Sydney to Victoria to raise money for crippled children. By the time he'd explained how he got the idea for the trip, how many tires he'd destroyed, how motorists reacted (some tried to run over him) and how he'd been received in various towns along the way, Ranse was almost overcome with impatience.

"Get on with it," he shouted at the screen. "Who gives a damn anyway? Roll that seven!"

Finally, the next celebrity, an actress with the most gorgeous red hair, got around to spinning her wheel. It stopped at seven.

"Now a three!" Ranse roared. "And I'll get fifty bucks at least!"

But before the next spin, there was an ad from a bank urging people not to let their lives be restricted for lack of funds when all they had to do was "use our money." This infuriated Ranse more than ever.

"Use your ruddy money," he shouted. "Oh yeah? And pay it back at twenty per cent interest, if you can manage to pay it back at all. Only people you'll lend money to are people who have lots."

Then there was a song, a goosed-up version of "Happy

Days Are Here Again," a long interview with the third wheel-spinner, a slickie who'd written a book describing how to make a million in the stock market, and, finally, the spin. As the wheel turned, Ranse kept muttering "Three, three, three," as though he could influence the wheel in his favour. It stopped at six. He had a six, all right, but it was on a different ticket from the two and the seven.

After that Ranse lost interest in the spinning, which dragged on for four more numbers, and this was followed by a long explanation of who won what. Then the whole process was repeated again for the second draw. This time Ranse didn't even have the first number right on any of his tickets. Josie went complacently on with her knitting, but Ranse began to figure out just how slim his chances were of winning anything. He tore up his tickets in a fit of rage, snarled at the unctuous master of ceremonies in the white suit, and told them all where they could stick Lotto Canada.

It was then that his great plan moved again up to the front of his conscious mind.

Everything seemed to make him mad these days: the twinge of arthritis in his right knee that warned of bad things to come, the thought of dwindling sex urges, the greyness of his beard, getting old generally. But mostly it was this damned inflation!

Every time it was mentioned on TV he would blow up. "Bloody politicians talking about ending inflation. Hah! They don't want to end inflation. They love inflation. Look at the money big business is making out of inflation. It's only us poor suckers, who have nothing to sell, who suffer from inflation. The rest of them get richer and richer!"

And Josie would get that alarmed look on her face that she always got when he blew his top and would pause in her game of solitaire (how that woman played solitaire!) and remark, mildly, that "After all, things aren't so bad. At least we own our own house."

"Sure, sure, we own this crummy dump. Forty-five years protecting other people's property and I end up with this!"

"It's a lovely house and you know it. Especially after all the work you've put on it. And we have the children."

Children. The difference between men and women. No matter how old she gets, a woman has an interest, a concern, a job, a purpose. Her children and her grandchildren. A woman never retires, never stops caring, planning, doing. Not so with a man. He's got to have something else to plan and do. If he stops doing, he's dead.

CHAPTER TWO

It was the twenty-first of June. A beautiful hot day, with the sun just about as high as it would be that year. Trees in full leaf, garden stuff coming along fine, lake at last warm enough for swimming. Summer had officially arrived.

And it was Ranse McGruber's birthday.

Birthdays. Each year they came quicker than the last. And each year, his birthday caused him to think back to the best birthday present he had ever had. That was in 1931, when he was in Grade Eight getting ready to write his entrance exams.

And entrance exams were something in 1931. Entrance into high school, a big step forward in education. There was a lot to be studied for those exams. Like the parts of the human eye. He could still remember drawing it and putting in the lens and the retina and the iris and the pupil and the aqueous humour and the vitreous humour. You never forgot those things. And the ear. He could still draw it. And the circulation of the blood. From the right ventrical to the pulmonary artery to the lungs and back through the pulmonary vein to the left auricle. He could see plainly the large diagram on the blackboard, with red chalk showing the arteries, and blue the veins. Health was a tough subject.

And geography (countries and capitals of South America and the counties of Ontario), and history (the Quebec Act, which gave the French Canadians the right to their own religion and language and civil law). And arithmetic (how to discount a promissory note and find the area of a circle and the volume of a cylinder). Grammar. Most kids don't know what it means. Eight subjects in all, and the exams came from the Department of Education and were returned there in sealed envelopes for marking. A real test, the entrance exams were.

And then that day, his birthday, sitting at his desk with the big flies buzzing against the windows and the smell of chalk and dustbane. Baldy Beckwith, the principal and Grade Eight teacher, would announce the names of the lucky ones who would be passed without writing. The kids squirming in their seats (not all the kids, of course, some didn't have a hope of being recommended) while Baldy acted as though nothing was afoot. A great sense of drama, not to mention sadism, had Baldy Beckwith.

And then, finally, the names had been read out: Dorothy Campbell, Sheila Hatstetter, and Ranse McGruber. Hot dog! Out of school a full week ahead of Puss and Jock and Skinny and all the rest of them. While they sweated and pondered in that hot room, he'd be free to go swimming in the municipal pool or fish in the river or just lie around in the back yard and listen to the birds sing. An extra week added to his two-month holiday. The greatest birthday of all.

And now he was sixty-one. The same sun shining, same birds singing. And he was the same person, really. You don't change with the years, just get more wrinkled and stiffer in the joints, and your eyesight dims, and your hearing deceives you. But inside. Inside you're the same person who felt a great surge of joy when you didn't have to write the Grade Eight exams. And a great feeling of anger and frustration when you couldn't go to summer camp with the other kids because in 1931 your parents just couldn't raise the money.

And, forty-eight years later, it was still a lack of money. After working his ass off all those years, long hours, getting all the overtime he could manage. And after raising his family and sending them to university and saving all he could and squirreling away a bit here and a bit there, he was still poor. His savings and his pension had looked pretty good until the price of everything had doubled, then tripled, and then quadrupled. What had seemed like a comfortable cushion for retirement was barely enough to live on.

He drove the Nova into Port Perkins to get his mail and do some shopping. They were tearing up the street again for sewers. And that meant higher taxes. He passed the recreation hall and the billboard for the summer theatre advertised *The Man Who Came to Dinner*–his favourite play. He'd been in it back in '54, playing Sheridan Whiteside. But the tickets. Six dollars each? To hell with it!

In the post office, Roy Alcock greeted him. "You should be a cinch to win."

"Win what? The fur-lined ice box?"

"No. The beard-growing contest for the Centennial in August. Most of us are starting from scratch, ha, ha. But you, with all that brush on your puss, you've got a six-month start on us."

"Yeah. Well, I wouldn't mind winning something."

He got the mail from the box. Telephone bill. That would be high with all the phoning Josie'd been doing to Helen, who was expecting her first child in Regina. Hydro bill. Probably another increase. Pension check. No increase there. Same four hundred and sixty-four dollars and eighty-five cents. Card from Susie in Toronto, with a picture of an old geezer on the front with lettering, I CAN'T FORGET YOUR BIRTHDAY, and then, when he opened it, there was a small cartoon of an even older geezer and the lettering, YOU LOOK TEN YEARS OLDER. Ain't it the truth. There was a note that said they'd like to come up for the July First weekend. Fine.

He drove down the hill and across the bridge to the one short business street of the town. No space on either side for more streets with the Wally River on one side and Lake Rondo on the other. He nosed the Nova into one of the slanting parking spaces across from the bank, crossed the street, and pushed open the heavy outer glass doors of the building.

As he did so, he noticed something strange about the doors. On the jamb of one was a little chain like the kind they have in hotel rooms that fit in a metal slot on the jamb of the other door. He paused for a split second and considered it. Funny thing to have on a bank door, but very handy for anyone without a key who wanted to prevent people from coming in. Ranse made a mental note of it.

He also, as he had for weeks now, studied the interior of the bank. Simple plan. Rectangular space with the manager's office at the front, its big window facing the street. Two doors to the manager's office: one behind the tellers' counter and one in front of it. And along this counter, which ran almost the length of the bank, were the three wickets, behind each of which was a female teller.

Ranse didn't know the names of these tellers. Each smiled a broad, impersonal smile whenever he approached, called him by name and asked him how he was. And he always said he was fine.

All except Madelaine, she of the long, raven locks who occupied the third wicket. Her smile was warm and, he felt, personal. After making out his deposit slip, he waited in her line, although there were shorter lines at the other wickets. And when he got to the front, it seemed to him that her face lit up.

"Well, Mr. McGruber, how are you today?" she said, coquettishly he thought.

"I'd be a lot better if you called me Ranse."

There was something about this girl that got to him—big brown eyes that seemed inviting, clear bronzed skin, full red lips. He felt his hormones stirring as he always did when he faced her.

She grimaced in mock surprise. "Why, Ranse, how nice of you!"

"I'm a nice guy."

"Yes, that's what I hear on all sides. Of course I have no first-hand knowledge."

Did she mean she'd like to have? But she had become all business, punching out his deposit on the machine beside her and then counting out the hundred dollars cash. "Have a good day." A dismissal phrase if he ever heard one.

As he moved out of the line, stuffing his cash into his wallet, Alec Parsons, the manager, motioned to him through the open door of his office.

"See you a moment, Ranse?"

Ranse went into the office. "What's up, Alec? Want to borrow some money? What security can you offer?"

Alec leaned back in his swivel chair and laughed, far louder, Ranse thought, than was necessary. He wanted something.

"Sit down, Ranse. Take a load off. Oh, shut the door first."

Ranse shut the office door and sat down opposite the manager. "What's up?"

"Well, it's this Centennial on Saturday, the fourth of August. All the service clubs are working together on it, and as the president of the Lions, I'm sort of involved."

"Yeah."

"As you know, the sixth is a civic holiday for other parts of the province, but we don't take ours until September, when the summer people have left and business has slowed."

"I'm aware of that."

"Which means," the manager went on, tapping his forefinger on the hard surface of his desk, "that because of the civic holiday there will be a lot more city people here even than usual. I wanted to have the mayor declare Friday a holiday, but the merchants objected that they'd lose too much money. I see their point. So we'll start things off with our beauty contest Friday evening and go through Saturday, Sunday, and Monday. We've got quite a program lined up."

"I heard something about it at the Legion."

"Well, that's what I want to talk to you about. The beauty contest. We need a man of your impartiality and good judgement to act as one of the judges."

Ranse McGruber was thinking. When you get an idea in your head, it's funny how you start relating everything else to it. Friday, August third: the town full of strangers; the bank full of money.

"Now I know it's a hell of a job," Alec was saying, "and you're not technically a citizen of the town, but we need all the help. . . ."

"What makes you think I'm impartial?" Ranse heard himself saying.

"Well, a happily married man like you."

"With no possible interest, personal interest that is, in any of the young beauties."

"Well, you know."

"Any of your staff entering?"

"Only Madelaine. She's the only one who's single."

"Okay, I'll do it."

"Great. I appreciate it." The manager laughed again and indicated, by shoving around some papers, that he had work to do. Ranse left the office and the bank.

He needed a bottle of scotch, he remembered, and the liquor store was down the hill on the highway, past where it turned at the end of the main street. The store was directly behind the bank, with a deep bush in between. Instead of getting into his car and driving around the corner and down the hill to the store, Ranse did something he'd never done before. There was a narrow lane between the bank and the next building, leading to the area behind the bank and the stores. Ranse took it.

Behind the bank was a path that led down the hill, through the bush, and came out at the liquor-store parking lot. The store was strategically placed so that it could be reached by boat or by car. On one side was the parking lot, and, on the other, a dock on the river.

Ranse went down the winding, seldom-used path, crossed the parking lot and entered the liquor store. It was a large log building with a walkway on one side and steps leading down to the dock. A sign on the door read, THIS STORE CLOSED TUESDAYS.

Ranse had always known this, a damned inconvenience, but all the government liquor stores closed one day a week. But why on Tuesdays? And, like the pieces of a huge jigsaw puzzle, that bit of information fitted into his plan.

He took his bottle of scotch (he allowed himself one a week) from the shelf, swearing inwardly, as always, at the recent increase in price. At the counter the manager of the store greeted him.

"You know," Ranse said, "you've got a great place to work. That view out there of the river and the birch and maple and the cottages. It can't be beat."

"Better 'n the place we used to have on the main street," the manager agreed. "That is, when I can see the view through the weekend line-ups."

"You'll have a lot in here the week before the Centennial."

"Don't mention it."

"I suppose you'll be closed that Tuesday as usual?"

"Yep. Thank the Lord."

Ranse paid the ten-twenty for his scotch and left. Again he took the little path up the hill and past the bank to the main street. But this time he counted the steps and timed himself. Nobody noticed him coming up the lane beside the bank. He resolved never to use that path again, until he really needed to.

Ranse was so preoccupied during his shopping at the IGA that he forgot to get any soda water. Driving home, he found his hands sweating at the wheel. That wouldn't do. If he were this agitated just thinking about the plan, how could he be cool enough to carry it out? One problem nagged at him. Toronto or New York? People knew him in Toronto. It would have to be New York. But how could he get there without anybody knowing? Especially Josie.

When he drove into the driveway, Josie was on the steps waiting for him.

"What took you so long?" she wanted to know.

Ranse could see that she was upset about something. "What's up?" he asked.

Josie was still an attractive woman. Small and compact, she hadn't got broad in the beam, as happens to so many grandmothers. She was, he decided, one of the few women over fifty who looked good in slacks. He loved her as much now as he had that day in 1942 when he'd first met her in the wardroom of H.M.C.S. *York*. And now, for some reason, the events of that night flashed through his mind.

Josie had come to the party with Lieutenant Ambers, the Number One, a young bachelor who had a knack for finding and dating particularly attractive women.

"Want you to meet Fearless." Ambers was more than slightly drunk. "Our intrepid provost officer. He's in charge of law and order around here. This is Josie." Then, noticing Josie's glass was empty, he continued, "Talk to him while I get you a refill. Mustn't let you go thirsty."

Ambers never let his dates go thirsty. Things worked out easier that way. But looking at Josie, Ranse got the distinct impression that Ambers was going to be disappointed this night.

"Fearless?" Josie asked, wrinkling her wide forehead with a pretty frown.

"Yeah, well they call me that because I'm a cop. Fearless Fosdick, you know."

"No, I don't think I do."

"You know, in the Lil Abner comic strip. The square-jawed detective that's a take-off on Dick Tracy. Fearless Fosdick."

She was confused. "And what's that got to do with you?"

"Well, you know, I'm a cop, a detective, and he's a detective, well."

"You are a real live detective?"

"Yep. I've been temporarily posted to this ship in charge of the shore patrol."

"I see." She smiled her beautiful smile that lit up her entire face. "I've never met a detective before."

"And I've never met anyone like you before, either. How come–?" He stopped just in time.

"How come a nice girl like me is here with a wolf like Lieutenant Ambers? I wonder about that myself. You can say I'm doing my bit for the war effort, helping to entertain our brave lads who are so far from home." Then, noticing his frown, "Oh, don't worry, I'm perfectly safe. I've been out with quite a number like Ambers and I've learned that they aren't so bad after they understand that, when you say no, you mean no. Besides"–she motioned towards one of the large chesterfields–"I think our friend has found, should I say more fertile pastures."

Ranse looked and sure enough there was Ambers sitting beside, or rather practically on, a voluptuous brunette who looked as though she had never said no in her life.

"You might just be stuck with me," Josie continued, with a little laugh that indicated she didn't mind.

And that's how it began. Later, they danced and Ranse held her very close. And he kissed her and she kissed him and Ranse McGruber, Provost Officer, was a dead duck.

He often thought of it afterward. Fate, that's what it was. He wouldn't have been at that party if he hadn't been on duty that night. And if Ambers hadn't happened to meet Josie . . . he hated to think of what life would have been like if he hadn't met Josie. She was the best thing that ever happened to him. Even better than getting recommended in Grade Eight.

Ranse often thought of Fate and its mysterious workings. And now it seemed to be pushing him along a road that no cop should think of following.

He thought of it even more when Josie said, "Ranse, I had a phone call from Regina."

"Helen?"

"Yes, and darling, I'm worried."

"Why? Something wrong?"

"Well, there is, kind of. The doctor says she might have to go to bed for the last two weeks of July and . . . ."

Ranse's head spun a bit. "You want to go there and help."

"Oh yes! It's her first one, and she *is* over thirty. It might·just·make the difference between . . . ."

"How long would you be away?"

"I'd really like to go and stay until the child is born and maybe a little longer just to, well, you know."

"You'd miss the Centennial celebration. Big things are planned. A beauty contest."

"Yes. Well, I'm sure they'll get along without me. It's you I'm worried about."

"Don't worry. I'll make out." His mind was racing. Josie away for the last part of July and well into August. "I may spend some time in Toronto and look up some of my old friends. I'm getting a little bushed here, anyway."

Things were working out. It was Fate.

CHAPTER THREE

He was walking down the winding road to the river, his daily two-miler, swinging his walking stick, his favourite walking stick that had been a present from Chief Damby.

Was he really planning to do this thing, he wondered, as he listened to the plaintive cry of the white throat in the treetop, "*Poor Sam Peabody Peabody Peabody*" and the raucous cry of the tiny oven bird, "*Teacher teacher teacher teacher,*" with the sun slanting through the oaks and maples, making patterns on the gravel road.

He heard a rustling in the bushes and stopped, lifting his binoculars to his eyes with his right hand, while at the same time removing his sunglasses and sticking them in his shirt pocket. He found a chipmunk sitting on a fallen log chewing away at an acorn. Busy little rascals.

In the midst of all this beauty and tranquillity could he, a peaceful man who'd spent forty years in law enforcement, be planning a violent crime? Impossible.

And then his mind reverted to his obsession, his paranoia. He was being diddled by the system that he'd worked to protect. It wasn't fair. Not fair that a few unscrupulous persons could manipulate things in such a way as to make themselves richer while making everybody else poorer. It made him so angry that he could take a gun and shoot somebody.

But useless rage, he knew, would get him nowhere. The thing to do was to plan every tiny detail so that there would be no slip-ups. As a detective, he'd learned that it was the little slip-ups that led to the identification of a suspect. From then on, it was just painstaking investigation.

When a crime is committed, it could be by any one of thousands of people. All those people, walking the streets, doing their jobs, riding the subways. All the same. And then some little thing made one of them different. And so the checking on that one person, singled out from thousands, began. And if he'd done it, you were sure to pin it on him, sooner or later.

So the plan was everything. Nothing to point the finger at Ranse McGruber.

No eyewitnesses? No, plenty of eyewitnesses, but all seeing the wrong thing. The more people around, the better. So, the Centennial celebration, when the town would be even fuller of strangers than usual. No doubt about it, that was the time. Tuesday, August seventh. Tuesday had always been his lucky day.

He stopped on the ancient cement bridge and looked down at the slow-running, murky water of Beaver Creek. A little higher today, which meant that somewhere, between here and the lake, the beavers were making another dam. It was only a few days since the cottagers had dynamited the old one. But those busy little beavers never gave up. Just as fast as humans destroyed their dam, they built another.

Everybody's having problems with the establishment, he thought. Even the beavers.

Well, he'd take Tim and Patrick in the canoe to see the new dam. They'd like that.

Dark water, dappled sun. Dark water, dappled sun. The rhythm of the words fitted the rhythm of his walking, and he momentarily yearned for the days of high school when life was simple.

Susie and Zeke and the twins descended on the house like a swarm of bees. Suddenly kids were everywhere and the house filled with laughter and shouting. As usual, the boys wanted to see everything at once. The tire swing that hung from the oak branch. They fought over who'd go first, and Susie settled it by having them draw straws.

Susie placed food and beer in the refrigerator. "We brought some steaks for a barbeque. I know we can't afford them, but after all, once in a while."

Zeke was busy carrying in suitcases and toys and depositing them neatly in the spare room. He was a tall, lean, athletic man, addicted to neatness, precision, and jogging. He was a good father to his boys, not through great affection for them, but because he knew the rules of good fatherhood and was determined, as with all rules, to live by them. He bought the boys things that, according to television advertising, were the proper things for boys to have. Above all, as befits a good cop, he was always fair and just and unprejudiced and even-tempered. But God help them if he caught them in a lie or any other digression from his strict code of behaviour!

"Take us fishing, Ranse?" Tim shouted, tugging at his grandfather's arm. He was half an inch shorter and considerably stockier than his twin brother. His direct, open countenance spoke of a straightforward approach to things and a direct course of action.

Patrick was leaner than his brother, with a longer, more thoughtful face. Although active and eager and reckless like any boy his age, he had his quieter moments and liked to investigate the mysteries of nature, such as the insides of a fish or the intricacies of an old oriole's woven nest that hung from an oak outside the front window.

"We'll take the canoe," he shouted. "I'll paddle!"

"No, I'll paddle." Tim shoved out his determined jaw.

"It's my turn," Patrick countered rationally. "Remember, Ranse, Tim paddled last time and you said . . . ."

"Okay, okay. You can both paddle. One bow and one stern. I'll sit in the middle and fish." And then, as the boys started to protest, "Or I'll sit in the stern and paddle and you two can sit in the bow and do the fishing."

"What about me?" Zeke asked, coming from the spare room dressed in a neat T-shirt and slacks, as befits a young man at a northern lake.

"Right," Ranse agreed. "Your dad and I will paddle the canoe, one at each end, and you two gaffers can sit in the middle and fish out both sides. Come on, let's go."

As they paddled around the rocky shore of the lake, on the side that was zoned open land and where no cottages were permitted, they went in and out of small bays, between rocky points, where no motorboats dared venture, and where, among the arrowheads and water lilies, fish of all sizes sought refuge.

The twins happily dangled their hooks, now and then bringing in a small perch or sunfish, while the adults talked shop.

"What about the Menzies case?" Ranse inquired. "Any break on that?"

Zeke looked straight ahead for a moment. Fishing or boating or swimming or golfing, his work was never out of his mind. "I've got a funny feeling about that one." He rubbed a big hand across his close-cropped hair. "It's too pat. It smells a bit phony."

"You mean you don't think she really was kidnapped?"

"Well, there's nothing to make me feel that. No evidence at all. The doc comes home, his wife is gone. There's a note on the table saying that she's been kidnapped and they'll get in touch."

"So?"

"And then we get the usual. Phone calls from booths and ransom notes. We bug the telephone. I don't know, it's like something out of 'The Streets of San Francisco.' "

"And you feel like Karl Malden?"

"God forbid! Those television cops. Easy for them. They've got the script writer on their sides, and the whole thing has to be solved within the hour."

"But you've got no script writer."

"That's the trouble, Dad. It seems to me there is a

script writer. Somebody planned the whole thing right down to the last detail."

Ranse felt something grip his gut. "You mean somebody besides the kidnappers?"

"Yeah. Suppose you want to get rid of your wife. Just suppose. You arrange a kidnapping. Everybody sympathizes with you. Perfect. But there's got to be a slip-up. There always is."

"Always?"

"Always. He's got to have an accomplice. Somebody is making those phone calls. There's the weakness of this perfect crime. As soon as you've got an accomplice, your plan isn't perfect."

Ranse's thoughts on this point were interrupted by a shout from Tim. "I've got one! A big one! Holy cow!"

"Watch him!" Ranse back-paddled to stop the canoe. "Don't let him get under the boat. You've got a pickerel on there for sure!"

While everybody in the canoe was engaged in the problem of landing the big fish, Josie and her daughter were discussing another problem.

"How do you mean Dad seems different lately?" Susie was asking.

Josie, standing at the sink breaking up a head of lettuce and looking out at the sumac in bloom on the rocks below the cottage, paused.

"For one thing," she said finally, "he let a television show go by without cursing at it."

Her daughter laughed. "That is a change. But as my dear husband would say, not much to go on."

"There are other things. I'll be talking to him and he won't be listening. Thinking of something else."

"We all do that. I understand it becomes more pronounced with age."

"Oh, I know. But when you've lived with a man for thirty-six years, you know when something is bothering him."

"I suppose so." Susie had thoughts of her own. Thirty-six years. Could she live with Zeke for thirty-six years? Such a long time with one person.

"And he hasn't lectured me about the age of confusion in months."

"The what of what?"

"Oh, you know. About how everybody is confused these days–about religion, sex, morality, crime and punishment. How he used to be sure of what was right and what was wrong and now nobody knows."

"I seem to remember."

"And how we don't understand what's going on. That lecture he used to give me every time he went to the bank, about how it used to be so simple and now only the computer knows for sure." She smiled. "I haven't heard that one for a long time."

"This is serious." Susie laughed, too. "Well, he's going through a change of life."

"And he worries so much about money and inflation. I tell him we have enough, and it just makes him furious." Josie wasn't smiling any more.

"You really are worried."

"Yes, I am. And I'm not at all sure I should leave him alone. I know Helen needs me there in Regina and I do so want to be with her, but, well, I suppose a wife's first duty is to her husband." She didn't sound as though she meant it.

Susie left the celery she was cutting and put her arm over her mother's shoulder. "A mother's work is never done. Don't worry about Dad. I'll try to come up and see how he's getting on. Helen does need you, and you should go."

Josie smiled, but she wasn't sure.

As he stood over the big stone barbeque that he'd painstakingly built, gently turning the precious steaks, Ranse McGruber thought of how long it had been since he'd sunk his teeth into a really juicy, rare piece of steak. This hunk here, he thought, must have cost over four dollars. Just for one steak. We used to buy a roast·for that, and it would do the family for almost a week. He added one small piece of seasoned maple to the fire below the meat. He never used charcoal. Hardwood was the only thing for barbequeing. Besides, it was practically free. Well, damn it, one way or another he'd have all the steak he wanted.

"This is so nice," Susie sighed, as they all sat down at the long picnic table on the patio. The sun was just sinking behind the tops of the huge oaks in the flat below the rock on which the house stood. "It's all worth the horrible drive up Highway 400. Such peace and, oh, everything."

The twins, one on each side of their grandfather, were actually quiet, as they stuffed their mouths with meat and potato salad and green salad and thought of the ice cream and cake to follow.

At one end of the table, Zeke meticulously cut his steak and made no comment. On the other side, Susie watched her father as she helped herself to salad. He did look preoccupied. He hadn't even asked the boys his favourite riddle: Why is an old maid like a green tomato? Give up? Because it's hard to-mate-her. Get it? The twins would always laugh, although they'd heard the riddle dozens of times. Oh, well, probably he was just hungry. Nothing wrong with his appetite.

When they'd finished their dinner, and the boys were still stuffing themselves with ice cream and cake, they sat on the patio and watched the sun go down behind the oaks.

"This is the best part of the day," Josie said, with the happiness of a grandmother with grandchildren around her. "When the sun is going down and the mosquitoes haven't yet come out."

Susie snuggled back in her wooden lawn chair, one that Ranse had built years ago. "It's so peaceful here. You're so lucky, you two, to have this place, far enough from the city that even the smog doesn't bother you."

Ranse got up from the table and walked around,

restless. Peace. Sure, peace. And boredom. The city may have its noise and smog and people, but there was always something doing. Always a new case to work on. The city was a place of problems, sure, but problems are life. Only the dead have no more problems. The dead and the retired. It wasn't just the need of money, he knew, that was causing him to contemplate this monstrous act. It was the plain and simple need to be doing. Planning. Figuring something out. Pitting his wits against somebody else's wits. You can't turn off the nozzle of a water hose. The hose might burst, and so might you.

"Can we go for a picnic on Rattlesnake Island tomorrow?" Tim demanded. "And pick blueberries?"

"No blueberries ripe yet," Ranse informed him.

"But strawberries," Susie suggested. "Last year we found a magnificent patch on the sunny side of the island. They're always a little later over there."

"I think that would be wonderful," Josie agreed, as the twins coaxed. "We'll pack a lunch and get an early start and stay all day."

"Can we climb the rock mountain this year? You said we could when we got big enough, Ranse." Tim was jumping up and down.

"I haven't had the motorboat out this year," Ranse said. "Don't know if that old Merc will produce another year."

"Soon see!" Zeke got up from the bench, glad of a chance to do something. He headed down the path towards the boat house.

"If it's runnable, Zeke will get it running," Susie said proudly. "That man can fix anything."

Ranse got up and followed his son-in-law down to the boathouse. That's what she used to say of him, he thought, as she stood beside his workbench in the garage. "Dad, you can fix anything!" And now she'd transferred that pride and affection to another man. Well, that's the way it went. The young take over from the old. Take over everything.

Rattlesnake Island was in the middle of the lake and un-inhabited. Other islands in the lake had their cottages, some large, some small, that could be reached only by boat. Each had a dock built out from the rocks and beside each dock was a motorboat. Big boats with hundred-horsepower motors. Boats that would make thirty miles an hour, or better, and pull water-skiers. Ranse McGruber had always wanted a boat like that. But the best he'd been able to manage was this sixteen-foot scow with the ten-horsepower motor. It was a serviceable boat, unsinkable, and would easily carry the six of them.

Ranse sat in the stern, handling the motor, while the rest of the family sat in the two seats amidships, with Zeke at the bow, ready to leap from boat to rock and secure them when they reached the island. As they putt-putted past the cottages, an early riser would wave from the dock, and Ranse would wave back. He'd have a bigger boat than any of them.

Rattlesnake Island was almost circular, with pines and birches growing on the steep rock face at the water's edge. The only beach was on the far side, in a little cove where the rocks were lower and the water deep. Ranse manoeuvred the boat in close to the rock face. Zeke leapt easily ashore and tied up to a birch tree whose roots found their way down into crevices in the rock. Then he gave a hand to each of the others, one by one, and helped them ashore. Ranse ignored the proffered hand and jumped onto the rock, feeling a slight twinge in his right knee as he did so. Damned arthritis.

Near the landing was a clearing, where years ago some energetic picnickers had built a crude rock grill. And beyond the clearing was the rock mountain, a huge, uneven pile of granite, with many crevices and caves. Over the years chunks had fallen off the side and were now covered with moss and lichens, ferns and small trees. At the top was a flat area, green with moss and some ancient pines that stood up, in silhouette, against the sky.

As soon as they were ashore, the twins started off through the woods towards the cliff.

"Wait!" their mother commanded. "Dad, do you think they can get up there? Is it safe?"

"Safe? Aw, Mom, sure it's safe." Tim shouted.

"How do we get up there, anyway?" Patrick asked, looking towards the craggy rock wall. "Do you know a way, Ranse?"

"Well." Ranse hesitated. He knew a path, all right, a narrow cut completely hidden by a low, spreading hemlock whose crown had been chewed off by porcupines. It was a crack in the wall that slanted up behind a huge chunk of rock that had been broken off, in earlier times, and that was invisible from below. Ranse had found it a couple of years earlier, completely by chance, when following a wounded partridge. So far as he knew, nobody else had ever found it, or, for that matter, been up to the top of the cliff. And now an idea had come into his head that fitted perfectly into the jigsaw of his great plan.

"Well, uh, I don't think there is a way to get up there," he lied to his grandchildren. "Tell you what, though, there is a great strawberry patch near the shore at the bottom of the cliff on this side of the island. We just follow this path."

"What path?" Tim wanted to know. "I don't see any path."

"Oh, it's here, all right. Kind of overgrown, but I can find it."

"Are there really rattlesnakes on this island?" Patrick had a great interest in anything that ran, flew, swam, or crawled.

"I don't think so," Ranse said. "Never heard of any this far east of Georgian Bay."

"Then why do they call it Rattlesnake Island?"

"Search me. Maybe to keep people away from it. Or maybe somebody did see a rattler here once."

"Have you ever seen one?"

"Yeah, I've seen massasaugas, but not in this area."

"Are they poisonous?"

"Very. But the massasauga is a small, timid rattler, and keeps out of people's way as much as possible. Come on, let's get those strawberries."

They found the patch, all right, and it was a good one. As the twins stuffed themselves with the big, lush fruits, Ranse sat on a rock and watched. Well, it's begun, he thought. The first lies have been told. How many more will I tell before this thing is over?

CHAPTER FOUR

"Whatcha making, Ranse?" Patrick wanted to know.

They were in the workshop end of the garage, where Ranse had been planing a piece of pine board. What he was making was a pine box, which he would line with tin. Then he'd put a tight lid on it, with a hasp for a small padlock. He didn't want the boys to know about this.

After the long weekend, Josie had offered to keep the boys until she went to Regina. Ranse wasn't so keen on the idea of having the boys for those two weeks, but he'd learned long ago that, where grandchildren were concerned, what Josie said definitely went.

"I know. It's going to be a birdhouse, isn't it, Ranse?" Timothy shouted.

Ranse wanted them out of there. "Yep, you guessed it," he agreed. "I know it's a little late in the year, but with luck we might entice a pair of cedar waxwings. They nest late."

"I saw one yesterday," Patrick said, "flying out over the lake and then back to sit on a branch. I knew it was a cedar waxwing because of the tuft on its head."

"That's right," Ranse agreed.

Ranse knew about that waxwing and its nest. He hadn't expected his grandson to be so knowledgeable about the bird. Amazing what ten-year-olds knew these days. May not be able to discount a promissory note, but they know a lot about birds and animals. All those nature films on television, he supposed.

"Can we help you put it up?" Tim wanted to know.

"Well, I don't know as I'll have it finished before you leave tomorrow."

"We'll help you finish it," Patrick volunteered, picking up a hammer.

"No, no, I don't think that will work."

These kids! So damned hard to do anything with them around. Hell, he could be building an atomic bomb out here in the workshop and Josie would never know. But with them around, he couldn't get away with building a tin-lined box.

Every little thing had been like that. If you're a family man, it takes a lot of scheming to do something in secret. He'd had a time phoning Air Canada for a reservation to New York. First he'd had to wait until Josie and the boys were on the beach and he had a moment to himself. Luckily, Air Canada had a toll-free number, so that wouldn't show up on the telephone bill at the end of the month.

Now, everything was set. Tomorrow he'd drive to Toronto, deliver the kids to their mother, take Josie to the airport to catch the plane to Regina, and, an hour later, at eleven o'clock, catch the plane to New York. This would give him more than a whole afternoon to do his business in New York before catching the evening plane back. And nobody'd ever know he'd been away, he hoped.

But that evening, with the kids finally in bed, Josie was bothered.

"I'm still not sure I should go tomorrow," she said. "It's such a long way." She had jarred the table and knocked his jigsaw puzzle slightly awry.

Have to be careful here, Ranse thought. Can't be too eager for her to go. Play it straight. How would he react to this news if it weren't a threat to his master plan? What if he didn't have a master plan at all? Without looking up from his puzzle, he mumbled, "Whatever you think best, dear."

She continued the argument with herself. "But if I

don't go and there are complications, well, I'd just never forgive myself.''

"That's certainly true, dear.''

"But what can happen? After all, in this day and age? The hospitals in Regina are every bit as good as those in Toronto.''

"Probably.''

"But still it is her first. Ranse, are you sure you can get along?''

"What? What's that?''

"Are you sure you can get along . . . when I'm away?''

"Always have. After all, I'm not helpless around the kitchen, as you know. No, I'll make out just fine. Miss you, of course, but it will be a comfort to know you are with Helen. Just in case.''

"I really don't know what to do.''

"Do what you want. Great thing about our present condition, we can do what we want to do. Within reason, of course.''

"Yes, that's so. Thanks for persuading me.''

"Uh? Yeah, oh sure. That's what husbands are for.''

When they were preparing for bed, a series of subtle indicators began to appear that told them that both were in the mood for love. After thirty-six years of marriage, you know those things.

As he lay with his wife, Ranse was overwhelmed, as always, by his love for her, and again struck by the realization that at least one part of a loving woman never grows old. And looking down at her eager face, he realized that in this position she looked as young as the first time they had made love.

It had been after a wardroom party. As easy and as naturally as any two married people, and each time it was a renewal of this first wonder.

And, suddenly, in that moment, he was overcome with the conviction that he couldn't commit the crime he was contemplating–couldn't jeopardize this thing they had. The risk of prison and disgrace he could face, but not the possibility of losing Josie.

Then, as he lay there in blissful contentment, his loving spouse, the joy of his life, the fount of all his delights, murmured sleepily, "Ranse, dear."

"Yeah?"

"When I'm gone you won't go chasing after some luscious young thing, will you?"

Suddenly he was dizzy with rage. How could she say that? Why would she say it? What a goddamned rotten thing to say. He could have strangled her. He turned on his side and humped his shoulders. His loving wife, totally unaware of what she had done, sank into blissful sleep.

The next morning Josie was up early, still mumbling about whether she should go or not. Now the twins were urging her not to go because it would mean they might stay longer at Wigwam Lake. It was now or never, Ranse realized. He'd managed to get enough money from his savings for the New York trip in a way that wouldn't arouse any suspicion. Although Josie checked their current-account statement every month, she really knew little of the savings account.

Then she made her decision. "I'm not going," she announced flatly.

"But you've got the reservation and all."

"That's easy to cancel."

"Whatever you say."

Well, that was that. Probably just as well. Somehow he felt relieved that he was out of it. And then the phone rang.

Josie answered it. "Yes, this is Mrs. McGruber. Regina?" Aside to Ranse, "It's Helen!" Into the phone, "Hello, dear. Yes, I can hear you fine. What's that? He did? Twins! Oh my goodness. How are you feeling, dear? I see. Well, don't you worry. I'm catching this morning's plane. Yes, I'll be there about twelve o'clock your time. Good-bye." She turned to Ranse. "The doctor says it's going to be twins! Oh, dear. She'll certainly need me now!"

A phrase from his navy days popped into Ranse's head: "diddled by the doubtful digit of destiny."

On the drive to Toronto, it seemed to Ranse that the boys were more obstreperous than usual. They argued and fought about everything. Finally, when Ranse stopped at the Texaco station, where gas was always a few cents cheaper, Josie got in the back seat with Patrick, and Timmy climbed in beside Ranse. It was a relief to get rid of them at Susie's split-level house in Etobicoke.

Susie had a little plan. Women always have plans. "After you drop Mother at the airport, come back for lunch, Dad," she demanded. "Then maybe you can stay here with us for a few days. Maybe see some movies."

Ranse thought fast. "Uh, thanks, dear, but not this time. I'm driving over to Hamilton to see an old war buddy I've neglected for too long."

"Oh? Who's that?"

"You don't know him. Slightly before your time."

"What's his name?"

Ranse was becoming confused. Why in hell had he said that? He could have said he needed to get home. What was his name?

At that moment the twins burst in, followed by Josie. "Hey, Mom, can we go to Ontario Place this afternoon? Art's mother is taking them. And she says . . . ."

This was a situation that completely occupied Susie's mind. "Well, I don't know. Four of you?"

"I think we better get going," Ranse said. "Traffic might hold us up. Come on, Josie."

There were kisses and good-byes and give-my-love-to-Helens and don't-you-worry-everything's-going-to-be-all-rights, and then they were on Highway 427 on the way to the airport.

Josie's plane was on time. Ranse got her ticketed and checked in and kissed good-bye, and then he was on his own. An hour until his plane would go. As soon as she was out of sight, he went to the wicket, bought a ticket and checked in for the flight to New York.

"Any luggage?" the attendant inquired.

"No. Just going for one day. Quick trip."

"Smoking or non-smoking?"

Involuntarily, Ranse felt his side pocket and his pipe. Then on impulse he said, "Non-smoking."

"Do you have a return reservation?"

"Yep."

"Very good, sir. Boarding is at ten forty-five. Gate seventy-six."

Time to kill. Ranse felt he needed a drink and made his way to the bar. It was crowded, but he found a small round table in a dark corner and ordered a double scotch and water. He was taking his first sip when a voice nearby shouted, "Fearless!"

He looked up and there, weaving in between the tables and making towards him, was a face he vaguely remembered. The portly man stopped at his side and extended a hand. "Fearless. I'll be damned!"

Ranse played it by ear. He stared at the man blankly and said, "What?"

"H.M.C.S. *York*, nineteen forty-three. I'm Boxly. Accountant."

Ranse remembered him now. How the hell had Boxly recognized him with the beard? "Sorry," he said in a gruff voice, which he hoped was disguised. "You've got the wrong guy. I was never at H.M.C.S. . . . whatever you said."

Boxly showed his confusion. "I know McGruber didn't have a beard then, but we met again at the Trafalgar Ball in 1952."

Jesus, so they had.

"What did you call me?"

"Oh, you know, Provost Officer. We called you Fearless Fosdick for laughs. I mean, uh, we called him that. You sure you aren't Ranse McGruber?"

"Positive." He laughed, as different from his own

laugh as he could make it, to show the ridiculousness of the question.

"Well, I'm damned." Boxly obviously wasn't sure. An accountant, he rarely made mistakes.

Ranse finished off his scotch faster than he wanted to and stood up. "Maybe you've had one too many, my friend," he said not unkindly. "Excuse me, but I've got to rush off."

The *my friend* might have done it, since it was a phrase that Ranse never used, detested, in fact, and the remark about too many drinks certainly would hit a sore spot with Boxly, who, in his wardroom days, had had a reputation as a toss-pot. In any case, he protested no more, but sat in the chair, obviously dejected.

On the plane, Ranse had another encounter of an entirely different kind. He had a window seat and the aisle seat was occupied by a striking young woman, obviously Asian, and obviously very nervous. Ranse pushed up the arm rest of the unoccupied seat between them, and suggested she do the same, to give them both more room.

"I never thought of that." She gave him a friendly smile. "This is the first time I've travelled on an American airline." She had a slight accent.

"Canadian," he corrected her gently.

"Yes, of course. Are you going to New York? But of course you are, since the plane is going there. Forgive me. I'm rather confused."

The stewardess, pushing her cart of booze down the aisle, paused at their seat. "Anything from the bar?" she asked.

"Would you like something?" Ranse asked.

"Why, yes, thank you. I think I would like a rum and Coke." Then, by way of explanation, she added, "I learned to drink that from the American airmen."

"Vietnam?"

"Yes. South Vietnam." This last was pronounced positively, so there could be no mistake.

"I see. I'll have a scotch and water. A double," he said

to the stewardess. He turned back to the young woman. "How long have you been in Canada?" he asked.

"Two years now." She took her drink from the stewardess and sipped it. Ranse accepted the two little bottles from the stewardess and poured them into a glass with water and ice. He didn't particularly want to pursue the conversation, but the young lady seemed anxious to talk. "It was terrible until we got out. But I was lucky. When I think of those boat people. . . ."

Ranse didn't want to talk about the boat people. He didn't even want to think of them. They weren't his problem. Come to that, they weren't Canada's problem. The U.S. had created it; let them solve it. Too many unemployed in Canada now.

The young lady seemed to be pondering whether to take him into her confidence. Suddenly, she blurted out, "I'm going to New York to meet a man. A man I knew in Hanoi. Knew him well. I was just a young girl then, and he was kind to me."

"I see." What the hell is it with me that makes people want to take me into their confidence? Ranse wondered. He reckoned that over the years he'd listened to thousands of personal stories. Don't encourage her.

But she needed no encouragement. "He came home to get married and I tried to forget him. But then I got this letter." She fumbled in her purse. "He asked me to come."

Oh, God, Ranse felt his gorge rising. Wants to have his cake and eat it. And so he's upsetting this girl's life. A life that's had more than its share of unsettlement already. Keep out of it, he told himself. It's no concern of yours.

"He's meeting me at the airport. Do you think I was a fool to come?"

"I don't know."

"His wife has left him. See, there, it says so." She pointed a long, slender finger at a line in the letter.

Ranse didn't read it. People did what they wanted to do in this world. Long ago he'd made up his mind on that. And they had to accept the consequences of their actions.

Long ago it had become his creed. How else could he have
arrested people for crimes if he thought they had no control over their actions. He applied the same rules to
himself.

Sensing his reluctance to counsel her, the girl stared
straight ahead, determinedly sipping her drink. When it
was finished, she surprised him by ordering another. He
let her pay for this one herself. Trying to get up her
courage, no doubt. Resolutely, he turned his mind to the
problem that lay before him as soon as he reached New
York.

When they were disembarking, his seatmate seemed
anxious to get away from him. Obviously didn't want
him to witness the meeting. But he did witness it. When
he got off the escalator that led to the departure floor, he
saw her stop beside a man in a wheel chair, a paraplegic,
and lean over to kiss him tenderly on the lips.

It made Ranse feel good. In some crazy way, he thought
of it as a good omen. In the taxi, on the long, tiresome,
traffic-ridden ride from La Guardia into the city, he asked
the driver if he knew of a good theatrical costumer.

"A what?"

Ranse repeated it.

"Well, I'm damned! I've been asked the way to Yankee
Stadium often enough, or even Grant's Tomb, but never
. . . yeah, I know one."

"Where?"

"On 54th, near Broadway. That's the theatre district,
you know."

"Yeah, I know. Take me there, will you?"

Good old New York cabbies, they know everything.
The taxi stopped in front of a narrow brick building sand-
wiched between two skyscrapers.

"This is one they ain't got around to tearin' down
yet," the cabbie said. "The place is upstairs."

Ranse paid him and went in, climbed the narrow stair-
way, and stopped before a glass-topped door with printing
on the glass that said, LEVINE–COSTUMES AND WIGS. He
pushed open the door and entered a large room filled with

racks of costumes. A bell tinkled and a small man hobbled from another room to the counter that ran across in front of the door. Ranse saw that he had one of those thick-soled boots such as a person with a club foot used to wear.

"Yeah," he said. "Can I do something for you?"

"I need a beard," Ranse said. In spite of himself, his heart was pounding.

"You got one," the little man said.

"Yes. Can you make me one exactly like the one I have? In every detail?"

"I could. Sure. But for what?"

"Well, it's a sort of joke I want to play on a friend."

"Damned expensive joke. A beard like that'll cost over a hundred."

Ranse was ready for that. "How long will it take?"

"How soon do you want it?"

"This afternoon."

"Of course. Why not yesterday? So you want it as soon as you can get it. Well, this is a quiet time. I can do it right away. Take a couple of days. You in the city?"

"No, I'm from out of town."

"I see. Very well, I'll mail it to you. Come in and let's have a look at you." He lifted the gate on the counter and Ranse went in. The man sat him on a chair, turned on some lights, and photographed him, left, right, and centre. "You want it exactly the same?"

"Exactly."

He made some measurements, fingered Ranse's beard, inspected it with a magnifying glass, and made some notes. "That's it. Where do you want it sent?"

Ranse had changed his mind. "What's the very earliest you could have it made?"

"Day after tomorrow. I just happen to have the right hair here."

"Fine. I'll wait. May go to see a couple of shows. What's good?"

"Well, the hottest ticket in town right now is *Sweeney Todd* at the Uris. Musical with Cariou and Lansbury."

"Yeah, I read something. Is that the one about . . . ?"

"Barber who cuts his patrons' throats and his girl friend who bakes them into meat pies."

"Pretty gruesome."

"But good songs. You probably couldn't get a ticket. Couple good long runs. *Ain't Misbehavin'* at the Plymouth. Fats Waller stuff. And if you want to go way back, they're doing *Whoopee* at the Anta."

"I remember the movie with Eddie Cantor. Any good dramas?"

"*Elephant Man* at the Booth, *Knockout* at the Helen Hayes. Get a *Times*. They're all listed there."

"Thanks, I will. Can I pick up the beard day after tomorrow?"

"Yep. I'll get at it right away."

Two nights in New York would strain his finances, Ranse realized, but he had his Visa card with him. He made a mental note not to let Josie see the bill when it came. He walked down 52nd Street to the Hotel Americana and was lucky enough to get a small single room. When he walked out again to get his *Times*, he felt good. Alive. He needed this change. Hanging around Wigwam Lake was making him stir crazy. He realized how much he missed the city. And action. A man of action can't just quit. Impossible. He noted the people on the street, tourists, businessmen, prostitutes, pimps, pushers. His experienced eye picked them out. Everything was there. Life. Action. Maybe when he got his money he would move to New York. No, Josie wouldn't like it.

Ranse had been in New York once before, in 1965, at a meeting of detectives from the U.S., Mexico, and Canada. He'd been on the drug squad then, and the meeting was to co-ordinate the activities of the three centres, Toronto, New York, and Mexico City. He hadn't learned much about the drug trade, but Josie and he had had a whale of a time.

Shows, that was the thing. Dozens of good shows on at one time. In Toronto then, he was lucky if one or two good professional plays were on at one time. Here, there were more than twenty. It was then he'd decided, or almost decided, to quit his job and become a full-time actor. From his Little Theatre experience, he knew that he was good. Maybe good enough. The euphoria had lasted until he got back to Toronto.

Then the reality of two kids, a wife, a mortgage, car payments, and dentist bills descended upon him and crushed his dream. He could have made it, though, if he'd had the guts to try. He remembered seeing Donald Sutherland in the local summer playhouse in the play *Bus Stop*. He hadn't been so hot. But look at him now.

Well, by God, he still had a chance for the ring. And, in a way, it was through acting. The success of his venture would depend on how well he could act. It would be the greatest part of his life.

He phoned Air Canada, changed his return reservation, went to one play and two movies, and, on Thursday, went to pick up his beard.

The little man hobbled out from the back. "Ah, the beard man." He reached into a drawer and produced the beard.

Ranse studied it carefully. Held it up to his face over his own beard. It was perfect in every detail. Colour, shape, even the little curl beneath the jowl. You couldn't tell it from his own.

"You like it? There is something wrong?" the little man asked defensively.

"Wrong? No. It's perfect. Absolutely perfect!"

"You know how to put it on your friend with spirit gum?"

"Yeah, I've had some experience with makeup. By the way, might as well get a small kit, now that I'm here."

"You're in Little Theatre?"

"Have been for a long time."

"That explains it. Good luck with the beard."

Ranse paid him and left for La Guardia to catch his plane to Toronto. In his seat by the window, he felt the headiness of the chase that he used to get as a detective. Now a chase in reverse. Instead of the chaser, he would be the chasee. No mistakes, no little detail overlooked. He had the beard. Now to make use of it without a slip-up. Pick the right moment. He looked out the window at the white confusion of clouds below. Everything was upside down.

CHAPTER FIVE

On the way back to Wigwam Lake from the airport, Ranse stopped in town for his mail and to do a little shopping. The mail was the usual bills, a letter for Josie in a hand he didn't recognize, and the *Weekly News Magazine*. On the cover of this was the picture of a balding man in an expensive suit, with his right hand extended as though rolling a dice, and beneath the picture, in bold type, the caption, "Gambling for Zillions." Ranse snorted his contempt, put the magazine with the rest of the mail, and drove down the street and over the bridge to the grocery store.

There he picked up some cheese, a frozen pizza, some Ritz crackers, a can of mixed nuts, and a bottle of club soda. (During the week before the crime, the criminal went about his daily routine without alteration.)

Then he drove up the street, past the bank, and turned the corner. He noted again the grove of maples and oaks between the back of the bank and the liquor-store parking lot. Two boys in shorts were riding their bikes down the path. Ranse made a mental note of it.

In the liquor store, a number of customers were making their selections from the shelves. He didn't recognize the girl at the cash desk. Summer help. From his office, behind a large window, Eric Peterson waved a greeting.

Ranse surveyed the shelf of scotch as he always did, ostensibly making a choice, but knowing that he would always take Dawson's Special, because it was the cheapest. And as always, his eye wandered over to the Chivas Regal and Ne Plus Ultra, which sold for eighteen dollars. Some day, maybe soon, he'd buy that.

At the counter he smiled at the dark-haired, very tanned girl, who was looking over his shoulder at a jock back at the wine counter.

"Hot day," Ranse remarked, and she smiled that large, vacant, thinking-of-something-else smile that young women reserve for the old. She hadn't heard him, he knew, and it infuriated him. He wanted to mutter, "Let's go behind some of those boxes and make out," and he knew that if he did she'd continue to smile and say, "Have a nice day."

When he drove down the winding road to his house among the oak trees, Ranse suddenly felt the weariness of his age. He parked the car beside Josie's Datsun and took his purchases up to the house. As he approached, he heard the phone ringing and hurried through the door to answer it.

Josie's voice, part worry and part petulance, said, "Where have you been?"

"In town. I just got home."

"I mean this morning and yesterday and last night. I've been trying to get you."

"Anything wrong?"

"No. Well, yes, in a way. I should really stay until the babies arrive."

Ranse felt a short surge of excitement. "Whatever you think, dear. How is Helen?"

"Big as a house, of course. And she's been showing. The doctor is keeping a close watch on her. He may put her in the hospital."

Ranse thought of Helen, his youngest. She always did things the hard way, it seemed. Babies. Why did women have them? God knows, with the cost of living the way it is they can't afford it.

"Well, you do whatever you must, dear. I'm okay."

"But where have you been? I've been trying to get you."

"Sorry. Outside a lot. Fishing, cutting wood."

"But in the evening. I tried twice last night."

"Meeting in town for the Centennial. Big doings, I can tell you. I'm one of the judges in the beauty contest."

"You?"

"Yeah. I'm a great judge of beauty. I picked you, didn't I?"

She giggled happily. "Yes, you did. And don't you forget it. You don't sound as though you missed me much," she teased.

"But I do, a lot. Haven't had a decent meal since you left. But I know it's important for you to be there," he added quickly.

"Yes, it really is. Well, this is costing money. Goodbye, dear. I love you."

"Likewise."

He heard her warm chuckle. It was an old habit, this love-you-likewise routine, and it always got him. He did love her. And he was responsible for her. Ever since he'd persuaded her that being a cop's wife wouldn't be so bad, he'd felt responsible. And for the girls, as they'd arrived, he'd been responsible. He was still responsible and responsibility was a terrible thing. What would she do if anything happened to him? He put the thought out of his mind.

Ranse got into an old pair of shorts, poured himself a drink, putting lots of ice in it, and padded barefoot and bare chested out through the sliding glass door to the patio. Thursday night. A lot of the weekend people were here already. He could hear the happy shouts of children in the water. All kids love water. But it was still quiet where he was. Lucky in his neighbours. No loud blaring outdoor speakers. Couldn't see a cottage in either direction. Far out on the lake, a small sailboat with blue and white sails was skimming along. A power boat, pulling a water-skier, rounded an island, almost out of earshot. He set his drink on the round table and sank back into the wooden armchair. Peaceful.

His mind went blank. It shut out thoughts of his jigsaw

plan, of the false beard nestling like a live thing in his briefcase. Everything.

"Yoohoo, anybody home?"

Damn, somebody was coming down the little-used path that led through the woods to the next cottage. What the hell was her name? He'd met her once. Nellie or Elsie or something with *E*s and *L*s in it. And there she was. A tall, angular woman of about forty, very tanned and slightly drunk.

Ranse got to his feet as she climbed the two stone steps onto the patio.

"That damned husband of mine," she panted. "Know what he did? Phoned from Toronto to say he couldn't make it this weekend. After me being here with the kids all week, and now he says he can't make it! Shit!"

Ranse didn't answer. He hated these frank, outspoken women. He hated women who swore and he hated drunk women. He'd dealt with too many of them.

"That's tough," he said finally, clearing some things off a chair so that she could sit down.

"Oh, I'm sorry," she said, sitting down. "I just had to talk to somebody over twelve years of age. Summer! God, how I hate it! Stuck in this place with three kids, three lively kids, I might add."

"Where are they now?"

"Down at the lake, swimming. With any luck, they'll drown."

Ranse couldn't help laughing.

"You men!" She smiled to dispel any notion of rancour. "Next time around, I want to be a man. Or a women's libber. Anything but a mother!"

"I think you need a drink."

"I thought you'd never ask. I see you're a scotch drinker. That will do me fine."

Ranse went into the kitchen and poured a drink. She took it, sipped it, and set it on the round table. "You used to be a policeman, didn't you?"

"Yes. Chief of detectives for ten years in Toronto."

"Boy, the stories you could tell."

"They've all been told . . . on 'The Streets of San Francisco.' "

"Do you like that show?"

"I like Karl Malden. First time I saw him was in New York in *Streetcar Named Desire*, with Marlon Brando and Kim Hunter."

She wasn't interested. "Where's your wife? Is she here?"

"Regina. Our daughter's having twins."

She made a face. "Poor thing. Poo-oor thing."

Ranse let that go and sipped his drink.

"Hey, I've got an idea. Now, don't think I'm one of those forward women, but I've got two lovely steaks over there; I was going to make a gorgeous dinner for that rotten husband of mine. The kids are going on a wiener roast somewhere. You're alone. I'm alone. Why don't you come over and help me eat those steaks?"

"That's the best offer I've had today, but—"

She laughed, interrupting him. "You don't talk like a man who's old enough to be retired. Now, my dad, that's retired. He's gone all to hell. But you–you're still in good shape."

"Well, thanks."

"What do you say? Choice steaks. Cost me over six dollars each. And I've got some Beaujolais that cost eight dollars, and . . . ."

Ranse was sweating under the armpits. He could feel the perspiration running down his side. How do you tell a woman that you just plain don't want to have dinner with her? Although the thought of the steaks was enticing, and the woman wasn't bad either. Little too tall for his liking, but well filled-out. Her breasts were almost escaping from her blouse. But no, thanks. He'd met this type of woman before and they were dangerous. More energy than running a house took, and so they drank a little too much. What she needed was a job that would keep her in the city. But how do you turn her down?

More perceptive than he'd given her credit for, she sensed his unwillingness. "I guess it's not such a good idea at that," she said, sipping her drink. "Tell me about being a cop. Were you on the take?"

"Not always."

"Did you have many stake-ups and shoot-outs?"

"You probably mean stake-outs and shoot-ups. It happens, but not with the regularity you see on television. If they made a show about what a cop's life is really like, nobody would watch it. Too dull."

She finished her drink and stood up. "I get the distinct impression you'd like to be alone. I see I can't seduce you–with steak, or anything else. I'll just have to go home and see if I can't lose myself in a good pornographic novel."

As quickly as she came, she was gone. "By God, I still don't know her name," Ranse muttered. But if there was one thing he didn't need, it as a nosy neighbour.

He heated up his pizza and ate it along with some lettuce and radishes from Josie's small kitchen garden. He turned on the television. A good show might take his mind off what he was going to do on Tuesday.

He searched for a show he could watch. Not much of a search, really, since his television set would bring in only two stations. But he was in luck. "Lou Grant," one of the shows that he could stand, was ready to begin.

As the credits flashed on the screen, he waited for the script writer. He'd always thought that one day his name would be there. It had seemed possible. He'd been studying drama most of his life. He knew about motivation and suspense and character. But he had learned that that just wasn't enough. Not one script had got finished.

Then Ranse became caught up in the play, which involved a Los Angeles killer named The Samaritan who, after five years of lying low, had written one of his typical letters to the newspaper. There was a strong possibility, Ranse figured from the beginning, that these new letters were phonies.

The beer commercial featured girls in white bathing suits and men in tight trunks diving into a deep grotto of clear fresh water. Ranse liked this commercial. One of the girls looked a lot like Josie had looked, thirty-two years earlier, when she'd had a bathing suit very much like that. And in 1947, when they'd bought their first car with the rehabilitation grant and taken a delayed honeymoon in the Canadian Rockies, they'd stopped at a mountain pool just like that one. And they'd dived and swum in water so cold it took the breath away. And then they'd made love and camped there for the night. Now she was old, as he was, and couldn't see well enough to dive off the end of the dock. Ranse got himself a beer.

In the last act, the young reporter who was working on the story tracked down the detective who'd worked on the case and who was now living in retirement on the shore of a lake. He looked like a retired detective, all right. And Ranse knew at once that he must be the guy who was writing the phony letters to the newspaper. It made sense. He missed the excitement and activity of the chase and wanted back in. Ranse studied the lean, wrinkled face of the retired detective. Living a lie, that's what he was doing. Living a lie.

But it turned out that it wasn't the retired detective at all, but a reporter who'd worked on the story five years earlier. And they caught him. He'd made the stupid mistake of using the new, revised edition of the Bible for the quotes that The Samaritan had always put in his letters. The Samaritan had used the King James version. So they caught him.

A stupid mistake. It was always the little, stupid mistake that tripped up the villain, at least in television plays. Well, Ranse told himself, he'd make no stupid mistake.

CHAPTER SIX

There are four factors necessary to the smooth and successful fulfilment of any project, Ranse read somewhere in a magazine, and they are:

1. Having a good plan, complete in every detail.
2. Careful and precise execution of the plan.
3. Improvising quickly and daringly to take care of unplanned contingencies.
4. Luck.

On the morning of Friday, August 3, as Ranse surveyed his bearded face in the bathroom mirror, he went over his plan. Was there any little detail he had overlooked? The disposal of the clothing was, perhaps, the most vexing problem at that moment, and, to some extent, this depended, he realized, on the fourth factor, Luck.

He rubbed his beard and the rest of his face. Not bad looking. Few wrinkles. A few little bumps that he couldn't explain. And the beard, grizzled and slightly curly, was magnificent. In a way, the entire plan depended on this beard, and the fact that no local person had ever seen him without it. Well, they never would.

Ranse poked around in the books in his so-called office and searched for a small yellow book he'd bought in his Little Theatre days. Must be here somewhere; he never threw anything away. Yep, there it was, wedged in between *The Art of Dramatic Writing* by Egri and *Televi-*

sion Writing by Greene. Ranse pulled it out and looked at the cover, *Stage Makeup Made Easy.*

He thumbed through the pages until he came to the section on beards, where he read: "A piece made by an expert wigmaker can be used repeatedly and will last for years." The book explained how to stick the beard on with spirit gum and how to remove it, and pointed out that, for a proper stick, the face must be clean shaven. That might present a problem. Time enough to think of that after he shaved off his beard, which would be at precisely two o'clock on Tuesday, the seventh.

The phone rang and Ranse went into the dining area to answer it. Probably Josie again. If she'd decided to come home early, the deal was off. But it wasn't Josie. It was his daughter Susie.

"Dad," she said anxiously. "How are you getting along?"

"Fine, Suse, just fine. No problems."

"Well, I know you're not one of those helpless men who can't boil water. Dad, the twins are after me to drive up for the long weekend."

"Oh."

"But Zeke has to do overtime. He's working on a case that he can't leave."

"That's too bad."

"And I'm tied up with a block action meeting. I was wondering . . . ."

"Yeah?"

"Well, the boys say they could go to Deepford by bus, if you could meet them there."

"Uh, hmm."

"You don't sound too enthusiastic."

"To tell the truth, Suse, I'm not sure I could handle it."

"But, Dad, you're wonderful with the boys."

"Sure, when you're here, or Zeke, or somebody they're afraid of."

"Dad!"

"Well, you know–two active, hungry boys, rarin' to go all the time?"

"Dad. This is so unlike you. Are you sure you're all right?"

"I'm fine, Suse. Just not as young as I used to be."

There was a pause on the line. He remembered years ago when he'd first realized that his father was mortal, getting old, slowing down. His daughter's voice came back. "All right, Dad. Their friend Art has been after them to go to Ontario Place with him. Maybe I'll let them go this time."

"Might be better. This town is going to be a madhouse. Besides, I've got some things to do for the Centennial."

"Oh? What?"

"Would you believe help judge the Miss Twin Lakes contest?"

"You? A beauty contest? Dad, really."

"Don't you think I've an eye for beauty?"

"Well, just watch it doesn't rove. But if you don't want the boys, you don't want them."

"I didn't say . . . ."

"Take care of yourself, Dad. We'll all come up later."

"Okay, Suse. Thanks for calling."

She was gone. That was that.

Ranse glanced at his watch. Damn, he'd lost fifteen minutes. He went out to the workshop in the garage and resumed work on the metal-lined box he'd been making. He fished out a pair of strong hinges from his equipment box, hinges that he'd bought a long time ago that couldn't be traced, and screwed them onto the inside of the box and lid so that they couldn't be removed when the lid was closed. Then, in the same manner, he screwed on a strong clasp to the front and fixed a padlock to it. Box finished.

In the afternoon, Ranse went back to town, making himself extra-visible this holiday weekend. He had a couple of beers at the Legion Hall and then watched the softball tournament. No referee had turned up and so he filled in for one game. Standing in his bright Hawaiian shirt in the hot sun, with the sweat running down his beard, he called the plays in his usual loud, deep voice for all to hear. A couple more beers before dinner, and then to the Presbyterian Church basement, where the Ladies Aid was serving a chicken dinner.

"You're having a busy day." He felt a hand on his shoulder and twisted around on the bench to face Alec Parsons, the bank manager.

"Nothing for a young feller."

"Well, save some of that energy for the beauty contest."

"Don't worry about me, or my eye for beauty."

Some of the ladies nearby smiled and laughed and wondered why it was they were seeing so much more of Ranse McGruber than usual.

The Community Hall was packed for the beauty contest. On either side of the door two huge fans droned in a vain attempt to keep the temperature down a little, but the place was stifling hot. Ranse and three other judges had seats in the front row, and in front of each was a TV tray with papers on it for the judging. Each girl was to be marked on looks, poise, and talent, and each would appear in a one-piece bathing suit, an evening gown, and, as a contribution to the region's growing fame as a winter resort area, a snowmobile suit.

Beside Ranse sat one of the high-school teachers, a young man with long hair and a beard and a flashy sports jacket. Beside him was an ex-hockey player named Gung Ho Gordo, a local boy who had played two seasons with the Toronto Maple Leafs and had been noted more for knocking other players down than for scoring goals. Since his early retirement, he'd made a considerable reputation for himself as a special guest at fall fairs, centennials, sports banquets, and the like. As the promoters of such events were wont to comment: "Old Gung Ho is always good for a laugh or two." The fourth judge was a woman well-known in the district for her water-colour paintings of local scenes, who ran an arts and crafts shop and had a justified reputation for knowing a touch of class when she saw it.

The bank manager was the master of ceremonies, and before the contestants appeared, he invited the judges to the stage to be introduced to the audience. Since he'd had a few stiff ones to bolster his courage for such a nerve-racking chore, he was, as they say, loose and humorous. After the guest of honour, Gung Ho Gordo, whom Parsons described as one of hockey's truly great stars, he brought Ranse forward and, clutching him by the shoulder, remarked that everybody in the district felt a little safer because of the presence in their midst of a nationally famous lawman, and from then on insisted on calling Ranse Matt Dillon.

Ranse smiled and waved tentatively at the audience, feeling the high he always had experienced when on the stage in front of an audience. He was playing a part, impersonating an upright citizen, a defender of law and order, while, underneath this benevolent façade, there lurked a cunning villain. In this respect, he had the prescience to realize that he was little different from the bank manager and his ilk.

Then they brought on the beauty queens. They came out in a line, dressed in their one-piece bathing suits. Leading the pack was Madelaine. She looked like an Indian princess with her heavy black hair hanging down on either side of her beautiful head in two long braids. Ranse had never seen her other than fully clothed, and the spectacle before him took his breath away. From her tiny feet and slim ankles to her rounded breasts, her figure was perfect. She smiled down at Ranse, and he was a dead duck.

Madelaine was followed by a half dozen other young women of varying heights and shapes. Some were local girls, others vacationers, and one was a rather well-known model from Toronto who had entered the contest for kicks.

They went through their routines of posing and smiling, turning themselves about and tossing their manes like fillies at a yearling sale. Then, while a local tenor belted out "A Pretty Girl is Like a Melody," the contestants got into their evening dresses and went through further poses. This was followed by the individual show of talent. Some sang, others danced, and one even recited a poem about her mother. To the surprise of most and the disconcertment of some, Madelaine did impersonations of some of the local citizens, including the postmaster, who had a decided tic on the right side of his face when he was computing the cost of a third-class parcel.

When it was all over, the judges withdrew to a small room off the stage to make their decisions. The school teacher came out strong for the daughter of the reeve. Gung Ho voted for the Toronto model, with whom, it turned out later, he was currently living. Ranse found himself being unusually voluble about the charms of Madelaine. The artist lady, somewhat bemused by Ranse's vehemence, gave Madelaine her vote, and Madelaine was declared the winner. The smile she gave Ranse more than compensated him for his efforts.

When he got back home after the contest, Ranse poured himself a good drink of scotch to settle himself, went to bed, and dreamed of Madelaine.

The next day, Saturday, he drove to town at ten and entered the horseshoe pitching contest. He won it, and had his picture taken by the local correspondent for the *Deepford News*. He smiled toothily through his beard. For lunch he bought a hamburger at the Lions' refreshment booth which he ate at a wooden table under the shade of an immense sugar maple. While he was sipping his coffee, Madelaine came over with a basket of chips in one hand and a coke in the other and sat down on the bench.

"I watched you pitching horseshoes," she said.

"You did? Must have been hard up for something to do."

"Oh no, I'm not. Since that silly beauty contest, I've been very busy. You know, pictures and stuff." Then she smiled with her full red lips and Ranse's corpuscles leap-frogged. ''Thanks.''

''No, no. I just called it as I saw it. You were, by far, the most beautiful girl there.''

What the hell am I doing here? he asked himself. Is this any way for a sixty-year-old guy to be behaving? And it's pretty cute the way you shaved a couple of years off your age there!

''Will you be going to the dance tonight?'' she asked, simply, without guile. She was referring to the monster dance to be held on the pier under a large, roofed-in section at the water's edge.

''Well, my wife's away and . . . .''

''I think it would be nice if you came.'' She got up, gave him another smile, dumped her empty chip-container into the trash barrel, and left.

In the afternoon there were swimming races and canoe races. Ranse had toyed with the idea of entering the latter; but when he noted the bulging muscles and flat stomachs of the young men who did enter, he was glad he hadn't. It was going to take a lot more than skill to win that race.

After the races, Ranse dropped in at the Legion Hall to refresh himself. At the bar he met Tip Tipton, who challenged him to a game of darts to see who'd pay for the drinks. Ranse couldn't miss, and beat his opponent easily.

''You're sure on a hot streak,'' Tip said. ''Horseshoes, darts. Everything's working for you.''

''It happens that way sometimes.''

''Yeah. You should try something big while you're on this winning kick–like robbing a bank.'' Tip laughed loudly. He was one of those guys who laughed loudly at almost everything he said, funny or not. Ranse laughed, too. It was a hell of a joke.

This, Ranse thought, has been a good day. He had really enjoyed himself, more than he ever thought he could. And this was a good community, and he was a respected and well-liked member of it. Then what in hell was he doing with a grandiose plan of grand larceny kicking around in his head? So what if he didn't have as much money as he would want? He could get a part-time security job and earn a little more. The warm sun, the friendly crowd, and the beautiful, orderly environment— that was reality. The rest was fantasy.

That evening, just to get some air and see how the dance was going, Ranse wandered down onto the dock. As he came down the hill beside the locks, he paused and looked at the scene below. Strings of brightly coloured lights reflected on the clear water of the lake. Men in shorts and summer slacks danced to a small combo at one end of the floor with girls in summer dresses. Ah, the girls in their summer dresses! The night was full of laughter and youth, something that had been missing from Ranse McGruber's life for a long, long time.

As he approached the lighted dance floor, Ranse felt a small hand slip under his arm. "So you came, after all," a soft voice whispered. *Her voice was ever soft and low, an excellent thing in a woman.* "Shall we dance?"

Something much akin to an electric shock shot through Ranse McGruber. The feel of her, the essence of her, was overpowering. He was as incapable of rational thought as a mutt following a bitch in heat.

He reached down, took her hand, and whispered back, "Why dance?"

It was very dark. There was nobody near. Before he knew it, he had taken her in his arms. She came without resistance, eagerly, and then he was kissing that soft, delicious mouth. She pressed her body hard against his and he could feel all of it. He lifted her up and kissed her again hard. She squirmed in his grasp and got her feet on the ground and, without taking her mouth from his, began to pull him over towards the soft, inviting grass of the park.

There was no doubt that he would have pressed her to the ground and pressed himself on top of her. But nearby a voice in the darkness said, "Here! Here's a good place."

Madelaine heard it too, and squirmed from his grasp.

"Later," she whispered. "Later."

And then she was gone, and Ranse McGruber was alone in the dark. And he knew one thing for certain. He had to have this woman. If he had to lie, cheat, steal or even kill, he had to have her.

CHAPTER SEVEN

August 7, 1979.

A phrase from an old radio show ran through Ranse McGruber's mind. "What kind of a day was it? A day like all days . . . ."

A day like all days. Except that this day would most surely change his life, just how much he could not know. The time had come. After months of planning and thinking about it, the day was here, the day when his big project would move from the realm of thought to the realm of action. It was a beautiful day, just as the days of the long weekend had been. The sun was coming up through the trees; that stupid robin was still singing. The lake was smooth and clear. Beautiful. Should he forget the whole thing and go fishing? Maybe, but not yet.

He finished his breakfast of Red River Cereal, milk, and brown sugar, cleaned up the dishes, and looked at the time. Half past nine. The bank would open at ten.

Ranse dressed himself carefully in his summer slacks and his Hawaiian shirt, which hung loosely over the top of his slacks, and carefully combed his hair and beard. He went out to the driveway and got into the Nova, which he backed out of the driveway onto Shorebank and headed for town.

After the holiday weekend many vacationers had gone back to the city, but there were still plenty of them on the street. This new crop, beginning their holidays and living in the lodges, cottages, cabins, or campgrounds of the area, were all preoccupied with shopping, gawking, and making plans. There were dozens of children among them, dodging back and forth on the street, ignoring the walkers.

Ranse parked near the bank and went in. The place was full, with a long line in front of each wicket. The lines moved slowly, for many of the customers–managers and messengers from lodges, restaurants, markets, souvenir shops, who had all done a big business over the holiday– were making their deposits from canvas bags full of bills.

Ranse joined one of the lines and noted that the worried woman at the wicket had removed a stack of bills at least a foot high, tied together with elastics. From the colour, Ranse guessed that many of them were fifties. Fifty-dollar bills, he thought ruefully, were as common now as twenties had been ten years ago.

When Ranse finally got to the wicket, he smiled at Madelaine, and she rewarded him with another big smile.

"How are you today, Mr. McGruber?"

"Fine, fine. You seem busy."

She grimaced. "Been like this since the bank opened and will be until just before we close at three. Please endorse this on the back." She shoved back his fifty-dollar cheque made out to cash.

"Sorry, always forget to do that."

She gave him the money and a sweet smile and he left. He took his fifty dollars to the supermarket down the street and bought some milk, eggs, cheese, bread and bananas, and one large steak which alone cost him four dollars and sixty-eight cents. At the checkout counter, he joked briefly with the girl, took his bag of groceries to the trunk of his car, and walked up the sidewalk to the drugstore. It was coffee time, and so he joined three men who were sitting on stools at the back. This elite group included Jim Bradshaw, the town mayor, Parsons, the bank manager, and Tom Wilkinson from the Sunlight Real Estate office next door. Tip Tipton, who ran the drugstore, was behind the counter.

"Now here's a man who has plenty of time and plenty

of money," Mayor Bradshaw quipped. "We've just got to find something useful for him to do around here."

"Well, we could use a policeman," Tipton said. "And they tell me he's had some experience."

The bank manager shook his head gravely. "The way they've been breaking into cottages around here . . . ."

"Yeah, it wouldn't be so bad if they just stole stuff," Tipton agreed. "But this useless vandalism, that's what gets me. Know what they did out at the Harding place?"

"No respect for law and order," Wilkinson said. "Should bring back the rope."

"For vandalism?" Ranse asked.

"Well, no, of course not. But it's all part of the same damned thing. These young punks know they can get away with anything. And what about those two young buggers who stabbed the girl at Deepford and then ran over her? Hanging's too good for them."

The three others nodded sombre agreement.

"I don't know," Tipton said. "We just seem to let people get away with anything these days. Judge gives them a pat on the wrist and suspended sentence. Should go to jail."

"And make real criminals of them?" Ranse asked.

"I don't know. Something's wrong. I can tell you that."

"Yeah, like charging forty cents for a cup of this swill," Bradshaw suggested, swirling the remains of his coffee around in his cup.

"I don't set the gawddamn prices. You know that! I don't notice anybody selling cars at the 1948 prices."

"Well, anyway we're all better off than we ever were," the mayor said, getting up from his stool. "I gotta get back to work."

"Now what in hell do you suppose he calls work?" Tipton said, wiping a wet spot off the counter where the mayor's cup had sat. "Now if he'd just do something about the lack of parking space in this town."

"Pretty hard to remedy that," Ranse said. "What with the town completely closed in by water."

"Oh there's space, if they want to use it. Found space for the liquor store all right," Tip added with a knowing wink.

"Well, yeah. Often wondered why they put it down at the end of the town like that. Of course, building it on the lake gives access to both boats and cars."

"Sure, sure. True enough. But there's other places. Down by the bridge for instance, on this side of the street. Of course, that land didn't happen to be owned by the mayor."

"Oh? Didn't know he'd owned the liquor-store property."

"That and all that bush between it and the main street."

Ranse felt a little twinge. "You mean that bush behind the bank there?" He was going to add, "with the winding path through it," but stopped himself.

"Sure thing. Now there's a place for a parking lot. Handy to the main street. Take considerable fill, of course."

"Any chance they might do it?"

"I've heard some talk. But the mayor's probably got other ideas–more profitable ideas."

Ranse paid for his coffee and left. He walked down the street, sometimes stepping off the curb to get around a group of visitors standing in the middle of the sidewalk talking. Trouble with summer people, he thought, they leave their manners at home with their troubles.

He stopped in at the post office and picked up his mail: a home-printed circular advertising cottage maintenance and a posh envelope from an outfit in Windsor that wanted to sell him German glassware by mail and a letter from Josie. She hoped he was getting along all right; Helen was due any day now; Herb was afraid he might lose his job with the government because of the austerity program. Just what he needed, when they were having twins. Ranse drove home in a bad mood.

It was lunch time when he got back to his cottage. All during the drive he'd been thinking, almost in a daze, about his plan. There was still time to call the whole thing off, to forget about it and go on living as he'd always done, living his peaceful, uneventful, boring, poverty-threatened life. He envisioned himself sliding into old age, peacefully and gracefully, gradually losing his teeth and his marbles, getting a little more feeble each month, losing the desire and energy to attempt anything daring. And then, one day or night, violently coming to the end of it all.

When you come right down to it, what did he have to lose? The worst that could happen would be that he'd get caught. Then what? A trial. With his record of good living and dedicated service, a minimum sentence, surely.

No, it was now or never. And the prospect of "never" made him sick.

From here on, timing was everything. The bank closed at three. He would hit it at five minutes to three. It was now eight minutes after twelve. Ranse made himself a bacon, tomato, and lettuce sandwich, ate it, cleaned up the kitchen. By then it was two minutes to one. He turned on the radio and listened to the Dominion Observatory time signal. "Ten seconds after the long dash, a long beep will signal exactly one o'clock, Eastern Daylight Time." His watch was a minute fast. He corrected it.

Then he went into the bathroom.

He stood in front of the mirror and surveyed his face. From a maple tree outside the window, the robin was continuing its monotonous chirping. What the hell for? he wondered. Not establishing territory. Nesting was long since over. In fact he'd seen a couple of young ones out of the nest the day before, hopping along in their spotted breasts, waiting for their mother to come back with a worm or a grasshopper.

He rubbed his full beard, still dark in spots, but showing a lot of grey. A full inch long on cheeks and chin. Then he took the scissors and began cutting the long hair of the beard. It fell in chunks into the basin, and he realized that it was most important to dispose of all those chunks. No little slip-ups.

After the scissoring, he took his electric razor, set it to trim, and carefully, beginning at the sideburns, drew it down his left cheek. The skin beneath was a sickly white in sharp contrast to his deeply tanned nose and forehead. He went down one cheek and then the other, then the chin, and, last of all, the jowls, neck, and the mustache. He set the razor to shave and went over his whole face and neck again.

The result was startling. In five years, he'd completely forgotten what he looked like under that beard. A complete stranger was staring back at him, a stranger with a lean, wrinkled, pale face, wearing a look of surprise and alarm. He'd forgotten the mole on his cheek, the slightly receding chin, the sagging jowl, the wrinkled neck.

For a long moment he stared at the stranger. Know thyself, Ranse McGruber. Was this why he'd hidden this face for the past years? The face of failure. The face he really hated, the face that for more than thirty years had snarled or scowled or grinned at hardened criminals and prostitutes and frightened kids and old bums. Come to think of it, he'd never liked this face. It wasn't him. Not Ranse McGruber, actor, writer, man-of-the world. A face with no character, a nondescript face, a nothing face. But it was definitely a face that no one would remember.

He gathered up the whiskers, all of them, placed them in an envelope to be taken out to the fireplace for burning. But first he opened his makeup kit, removed a small jar and smeared artificial tan on his cheeks, upper lip, chin, and neck. That looked better.

Then he heard it. A car in the driveway! Now who in hell . . . ? For a quick moment he panicked. A truck door slammed, and heavy steps came up the stairs. A banging on the screen door. Too late to get his artificial beard. The kitchen door was open, and through it whoever was there could see the bathroom door.

"Ranse!" He recognized the voice of Jim Hopkins from

down the lake. "Ranse! You in there?" A pause. More banging. "Old bugger must be out fishing."

Then he heard footsteps on the screened-in veranda. The nosy old bastard was coming in!

"Ah, there it is. My chain saw. I'll take it and let him worry about where it went."

The screen door slammed and the footsteps retreated down the stairs. The door of the pickup banged shut and the engine started. Ranse McGruber was sweating.

His actions now took on an unreality, as though he were in a play, compelled by a force outside himself to go through the movements and read the lines assigned to him.

First the get-up. Ranse put on his slacks and sports shirt again. Then he went into the bedroom and, from a back shelf of the clothes closet, dug out a rumpled pair of coveralls and the ragged slouch hat he'd used when he played the rube brother in the play *Our Mr. Bean.* He pulled the coveralls on over his clothes, completely covering them, placed the ragged hat on his head and surveyed the result. He looked something like the comedian Gordie Tapp of the "Hee Haw" show, but nothing at all like Ranse McGruber. For good measure, he took his makeup and drew a long, ugly scar from his ear to his jaw. The beard would hide it.

He had planned his footwear carefully. There just might be someone in the bank who would notice boots. Normally, Ranse wore a pair of moccasin-type slippers. Instead of these, he put on a pair of rubber boots that he'd bought in the city and never worn. A pair of large dark glasses completed the disguise. The most important detail would be to assume a slouching gait, in direct contrast to his usual upright posture.

Next step. He went to his gun case and removed the small hand gun he'd always carried as a detective, loaded it with blank cartridges, and slipped it into the large side pocket of the coveralls. Now this crude, bumbling rube was ready to rob a bank. All that remained was to get into the bank, commit the act, get out with the money, and resume his proper identity.

Then Ranse McGruber, ex-upholder of law and order and fighter of crime in all its aspects, removed the coveralls, hat, glasses and rubber boots, rolled them up neatly and placed them inside a Glad garbage bag. He attached the artificial beard to his face with transparent tape. No one would get a close look at his face until after the act. Next he rummaged in the drawer of Josie's vanity, picked up her purse mirror, and put it along with the tube of spirit gum in his pocket. Then he checked his face in Josie's magnifying mirror and noted with satisfaction that the beard looked okay and covered the scar. Nothing of the gawky rube remained. Staring back at him was a lean, athletic man with a longish beard and carefully combed hair.

It was now fifteen minutes after two.

He took the Glad bag out to the Nova and stowed it under the front seat, got in and drove to town. There were still plenty of people on the main street, making lots of noise. He drove to the end, around the corner and down the hill to the liquor store parking lot.

Forty-eight minutes after two.

He was in luck. Although the store was closed, there were five cars in the lot and nobody in any of them. Most important, the spot he wanted, right at the end of the store and against the bush, was empty. He backed his car into the space so that the trunk was right at the end of the path. Still nobody came into the lot. He pulled his bag out from under the seat and slipped into the bush, where it was almost dark because of the deep shade. He went along the winding path to the spot he'd marked, stepped off the path, and, behind a big oak tree, pulled on the coveralls and zippered them to the neck, and put on the soft hat. He removed his mocassins and shoved them under some twigs, slid his feet into his rubber boots, and, in a matter of seconds, was back to the path. He rolled up the garbage bag and stuffed it into one of the large pockets of the coveralls. In the other he had the gun.

It was now eight minutes to three.

He walked along the path, up the lane between the bank and the real-estate office, around the corner, and through the outer glass doors of the bank. He slipped the chain lock into place and pulled down the blind, as he'd seen the manager do. Nobody noticed. Then he went through the second glass door into the bank.

There were still three customers in the bank, a young man of about twenty in T-shirt and shorts, an old lady at the side table making out a deposit slip, and an ancient man at one of the wickets.

Ranse observed all this as he stepped, unnoticed, through the door of the manager's office. Holding his revolver so that no one on the street could see it, he pointed it straight at Parson's head and said in a low voice, "Push your chair back carefully, and stand up without touching anything, or you're a dead man."

Parsons stared at him blankly and did as he was told. Ranse stepped around the desk, shoved the revolver hard against the manager's back and pushed him towards the door that led out behind the counter. The girls, busy at their wickets, didn't glance his way.

"All right, everybody," Ranse said in a loud, phony voice, waving the gun for all to see, "just do what you are told and nobody won't get hurt."

The two elderly people looked up, dazed. Not seeing or hearing too well, they weren't sure what was going on. The twenty-year-old caught on at once, and looked as though he might spring into action. The three tellers turned their heads sideways.

"Please step back and don't touch anything," the manager said. "It isn't worth it."

The young athlete made a quick movement towards the door and Ranse fired a blank shot over his head. He stopped immediately. The noise from the street–trucks, cars, horns and people–would deaden the noise of the shot, Ranse hoped.

"Okay, all of youse," he shouted in his high voice. "Everybody on the floor, face down. You clerks, step out where I can see you."

The old people still stared dumbly.

"Do as he says," Parsons pleaded. "And please, no heroics!"

Customers and staff got onto the floor. "If anyone moves, I shoot the manager," Ranse said. Nobody tried.

"Now, very carefully, empty all these drawers of money."

Ranse pulled his garbage bag from his pocket and handed it to Parsons. Down the line they went, emptying the drawers of bills, but there didn't seem to be much. Then Ranse noticed the manager glance at the floor. Under the counter was a white canvas sack full of something that was obviously on its way to the vault when he came in. "That, too," he ordered.

Parsons shrugged resignedly and placed the heavy sack in the green bag. Ranse rolled it into a tight bundle and tucked it under his left arm.

"That's it," he said. "You, out front and on the floor," he ordered Parsons. The manager did as he was told. Ranse backed towards the front door, removed the chain, pocketed his revolver and, matter of factly, stepped into the street. A group of tourists were exchanging greetings in front of the bank, and had no eyes for him. Four steps took him to the edge of the bank and around the corner. He walked quickly down the narrow lane and stepped into the woods. Once there, he ran, unseen, down the winding path to his friend, the oak tree. He removed his coveralls, hat and rubber boots and shoved them into the bag on top of the money. Then he stepped into his moccasins, took his false beard from the pocket of his slacks, and, with the aid of his mirror, carefully stuck it to his face.

Quickly, he walked down the rest of the path to the parking lot. The rear end of his car was almost hidden in the bushes. Now he needed some luck. Farther down the lot, a car had just pulled in. The occupant, who obviously didn't know the store was closed, disappeared along the boardwalk that led to the door.

Ranse lifted the lid of his trunk, shoved in his garbage

bag, got into the car and carefully drove out of the parking lot. At the entrance, a pickup truck with a bearded giant and wild-looking companion wheeled into the lot without looking to see who was in the way. Ranse braked quickly and missed the truck by inches. Then he drove out onto the highway and made a right turn onto the main street.

It was full of cars, all stopped, all honking their horns. As he rounded the corner, a lot of people, including the bank manager, were in front of the bank waving and shouting. Ranse stopped his car.

"What's up?" he shouted to Parsons through the open window on the right side.

"We've been robbed, Ranse! A little fat guy in overalls just robbed the bank! I didn't see it, but they say he got away in a yellow car."

"No, it was a green car," a portly tourist in Bermuda shorts corrected him. "It went that way." He pointed down the hill towards the bridge.

"No, George," his wife corrected him. "It was a black car. A long one. And it went around the corner there."

Ranse heard the siren of a police car far down the street, but with the traffic jam, there was no way the police could get within blocks of the bank.

"Jesus, what a mess!" Parsons said. "Ranse, can you help clear out some of these cars?"

"I'll try." Ranse pulled his car to the curb in front of a fire hydrant and got out, locking the door. "All right, everybody off the street," he shouted in a voice of authority. "Move away, please, so that the cars can get through. Come on, Alec, let's get out onto the street."

The two of them went to the middle of the street and began moving the cars along. But it was a long, slow process, as cars were coming into the street at both ends and there were no side roads to turn into.

"Somebody get down at the bridge and stop any more cars coming," Ranse shouted. Other businessmen were now helping to take charge, and within ten minutes it was possible to get a car up the street.

When the OPP officer arrived, Parsons took him into the bank. Ranse heard him say, "We got a good description, that's certain!"

Ranse returned to his car and joined the line heading down the hill. Slowly he crossed the bridge over the locks and started up the hill on the other side. In front of the municipal office a police cruiser was parked, and the uniformed officer was holding up his hand to stop cars.

Now we are into point four, Luck, Ranse thought, as he pulled the Nova over onto the gravel shoulder. If he knew the officer it would be easy; if not . . . .

The officer was young, wearing sunglasses, and Ranse had never seen him before. As the officer approached the car from the front, he noted the licence number. Ranse stuck his head out the window.

"Can I be of any assistance, officer?" he asked in a loud, clear voice.

"Assistance?" The young man looked at him in some surprise.

"Yes. I'm Ranse McGruber. Chief detective for Metropolitan Toronto, retired."

"Oh. Yeah. Sorry I didn't recognize you, sir."

"This looks like a bad one."

"We'll get him. Can't have gone far. Witnesses saw him drive off this way in a car. Usual confusion about the colour and licence number. We'll put roadblocks between here and Deepford."

"Can I do anything?"

"No, thanks. Not right now. We've got everything pretty well covered."

"Well, good luck!"

The young man waved him on and walked up to the car behind him. Ranse pressed the accelerator and eased out into the traffic leaving town. There was as yet no roadblock at the entrance of sideroad 75, which led through the bush to his side of the lake. He met only a couple of cars on the road, and when he turned down Shorebank Road it was, as usual, empty. He pulled down his winding driveway through the trees and parked in front of his garage. Save for the sound of an oven bird shouting his endless *"teacher-teacher-teacher-teacher,"* all was silence.

Ranse McGruber shut off his engine and sat in the front seat and now, for the first time, he began to shake. He'd done it, but what if he hadn't? What if they'd searched his car? What if there'd been somebody on the path? What if somebody'd seen him in the liquor-store parking lot? My God, maybe somebody did and wouldn't put it all together until he heard the story of the robbery. It was so easy to put together once you had a clue. He found himself thinking of the robbery as a detective. One clue was all that was needed. One little clue.

One thing he knew for certain. His life had changed irrevocably. He had crossed over into the murky world of the criminals, the forever wary, the dissemblers, the hunted.

CHAPTER EIGHT

It was four o'clock in the afternoon when Ranse
McGruber pulled into his own driveway on Wigwam
Lake with his car full of money. He got out of the car,
removed the green bag from the trunk, took it into the
garage and closed and locked the door behind him. The
only light came from a small window on the side, and so
he turned on the electric bulb that hung naked above his
workbench. He was ready.

He removed the coveralls, hat, and rubber boots from
the bag and dumped the money out onto his workbench.
A pile of money, new bills and old, fifties, twenties, tens,
fives, and ones.

For a moment he stood staring at it, almost mesmer-
ized by its presence. Money! More than he had ever seen.
The stuff that makes the world go around, that people
spend their whole lives working for, that people lie for,
cheat for, betray their best friends for. Money, the stuff
that makes the difference between existing and living. He
had a wild impulse to bury himself in it the way kids bury
themselves in dry leaves, or the way a cat rubs it face in
catnip. But there were more practical things to be done.

First he counted it, arranging it in neat piles according
to denomination as he did so. And when he was finished,
he had $216,372 in cash! My God, he was a rich man!

Ranse knew that disposing of this much money would
not be easy, but he had a plan. When the heat was off,
maybe in the spring, he would begin taking given

amounts of the money to Toronto, and opening accounts in small neighbourhood branches of different banks under, of course, fictitious names. Once he had it on paper instead of in cash, he could gradually transfer amounts to one account. It would take time and patience, he knew, but he had it all worked out.

He put on a pair of tight gloves and carefully packaged the money in plastic bags and fitted them into the metal-lined box he had made for the purpose. Then he closed the lid and locked it with the padlock, and shoved the key into a crack in the wall and covered it with plastic wood. It blended perfectly into the pine board.

He knew where he would hide the box, but he couldn't go there until late at night. For the meantime, he took it into the woods, dug a shallow grave, and placed the box in it. Then he completely covered the spot with dried leaves and sticks.

It was eleven minutes to five, and he was ready for the next step. He took the coveralls, hat, and rubber boots out of the garage and over to his huge stone grill on the side of the patio. He placed the clothing in the firebox and stood contemplating the boots. Burning rubber would make a stink that would permeate the entire side of the lake and hang it the windless air for hours, perhaps days. The boots were new, looked like any other boots, there was no tell-tale earth sticking to the soles. He would return them to the back of his clothes closet. Then he placed the coveralls and hat in the firebox, sprinkled them with charcoal lighter, placed a goodly amount of seasoned oak and maple sticks on top and lit it. The flames shot up, as the dry kindling caught. Soon, all the evidence would be ashes.

Then Ranse McGruber went into his bar and poured himself a hefty scotch and water, brought it back to the patio, and sat back in his easy chair and watched the fire. From time to time, he got up, put more hardwood on the flames, and finally let it burn down to a bed of coals on which he would cook his steak. By that time the sun was down below the tops of the pines. He poured himself another scotch and sat down to enjoy his steak. He was very hungry.

As he drank and ate, Ranse didn't think of the money or the fact that he was now a criminal, or of his wife, Josie, or of his children or grandchildren. He thought of Madelaine–firm breasts pressed against his chest, soft mouth covering his, darting tongue exploring. A long, long time since he'd been kissed like that; in fact, he'd never been kissed just like that. How could he see her again? Phone her? Go in to the bank? He fingered his false beard.

The beard. He got out of his chair and went into the bathroom, turned on the light, and inspected his face in Josie's magnifying mirror. Perfect. Even at this distance, he could scarcely tell it was a false beard. And no one would ever get this close to him.

When he came out, only a few coals remained in the firebox. He poured some water over them and poked around until he found the long zipper from the coveralls. Everything else had completely disappeared. He dried the zipper off and placed it in his pocket. He knew what to do with it.

Six forty-seven. He still had over five hours before his next move. He went into the house and turned on the television set. "Hollywood Squares." He forced himself to sit still and watch it. Peter Marshall quoted an article from a magazine Ranse had never heard of that dealt with marriage problems, and asked George Gobel how many affairs, according to a survey, the average married man had.

"You mean in his whole life?" Gobel asked. "That's all kinds of men? The average?"

"Yes."

"Well, I'll tell you, Peter, when they asked me I lied."

Marshall laughed and repeated the question.

Gobel became thoughtful and said, "Two."

The answer was twenty.

Ranse thought of this for a while, realizing that he had about fifteen to go before he could consider himself a virile, macho, American male. Imagine that. Twenty! It made him feel downright steadfast. It almost made him think of Madelaine. Would he ever stop thinking of her?

"Hollywood Squares" was followed by a rerun of the "Mary Tyler Moore Show." The episode was about a pretty young girl who had come to the big city to make her mark in television. Completely unscrupulous, she made a play for Ted Baxter, Lou Grant, and the producer of Sue Anne's cooking show. Ranse could see what she was up to, all right. It's a bugger how a girl on the make can make a fool of anybody. But she got her come-uppance in the end, and all was serene at the television station again.

This was followed by a football game between Montreal and Winnipeg. Ranse loved football, having played guard in high school, but this one just couldn't hold his interest. He tried to get worked up about Winnipeg, who hadn't yet won a game (Montreal, as usual, was at the top of the league), but he couldn't manage it. In fact, he couldn't stay awake. The stress of the day and the let-down, followed by two double scotches, was too much for him. He dozed off in his chair.

When he came to, the game was just about over. For a second, he sat blinking, and wondering if he had dreamed the whole thing. No, it was real all right, and he, Ranse McGruber, stalwart upholder of the law, was a bank robber.

The game ended in a win for Montreal and the local news came on. The story of the robbery took up most of the newscast. There were pictures of the bank and a clip of an interview with the manager. In the face of the television cameras, Alec added a few embellishments that surprised even Ranse. Then they interviewed a tourist who had seen the robber get into a green pickup and drive away. Next up was a member of the Provincial Police, and he said that they had several leads that they couldn't discuss right now, but an arrest was expected momentarily.

This brought Ranse up with a jerk and reminded him

that he still had work to do. First, he put on his dark blue windbreaker and a pair of brown trousers. Then he put on his gloves, took his flashlight, went out into the woods, got his box of money, and took it down to the dock. It was a pitch-dark night, but gradually, as his eyes became accustomed to it, he could make out the dim shadow of the shoreline, dotted here and there with lights from cottages. Necessary landmarks. No sound of a motorboat on the lake.

Ranse placed the box in his canoe and shoved off. Silently, he paddled out of his little bay towards Rattlesnake Island. There was just enough light to enable him to find his way. Now if some late reveller didn't decide on a midnight cruise, he'd be home free. But most of the revelling types had gone back to the city after the holiday, and Ranse paddled the mile and a half to the island without encountering anybody. Into the dark, deep water in the middle of the lake he dropped the metal zipper and the remaining blank cartridges.

He beached the canoe in the little cove, the great trees and cliff looming above him, and lifted his box ashore. He tied a handkerchief over the face of the light, and by its dim illumination, found his way to the secret path and up the side of the cliff. He found the cave he'd noticed before, completely obscured by a mat of foot-high juniper bush–brush which would be just as lush in fall as it was now. Carefully he parted the juniper, and there was a natural cave about a foot wide and two feet deep. Ranse shoved his precious box far into the cave. Then he gathered dead sticks and other debris and shoved them into the mouth of the cave, hiding the box. Lastly, he found a flat rock, which he could barely lift, and placed it on top. Then he carefully pushed the tough juniper bushes back into place. There was nothing to indicate that they'd ever been disturbed. His treasure was safe for as long as he wanted to leave it there.

Back in his cottage, Ranse poured himself a large drink and sat nursing it. No evidence. Nothing to connect him with the crime. No accomplice to blab. Unless someone had noticed him in the liquor-store parking lot, nobody would ever suspect him. And even then they couldn't prove he hadn't been there innocently. He had accomplished the perfect crime. He finished his drink and went to bed. The crazy saying ran through his mind: "Today is the first day of the rest of your life."

Next morning Ranse awoke with an itchy face. He went into the bathroom and with rubbing alcohol removed his false beard. Underneath, his face had a stubble of whiskers and was very sore. Before he had figured out what to do about it, the phone rang.

Josie? Saying she was coming home? Let it ring? No, he couldn't do that. Might be an emergency. Quickly he reached for his beard, and then had to laugh out loud. Putting on a beard to answer the phone. He hurried into the dining area and picked it up.

"Hello."

"Hello, Dad?"

"Yeah, Susie. It's me."

"How are you getting along?"

"Fine. Just fine. Putting on weight."

"Are you sure, Dad?"

"No, not actually, but I'm doing okay. Been a lot of excitement around here."

"So I heard on the radio. Have they caught the bank robbers?"

"Not that I've heard."

"Well, they will. Listen, Dad, we're thinking of driving up next weekend. Will that be okay?"

Here it was. The complication of family. He thought furiously. And Zeke. Oh yes, Zeke.

"Dad? Are you still there? Did you hear what I said?"

"Yeah. I heard. There's just one thing."

"What's that?"

"Well, I promised to take a guy fishing up to the park next week, starting Friday. Don't see how I can get out of it."

"Oh." Her voice was full of disappointment.

"But you can use the place if you want." His mind was

clicking. Yeah, a fishing trip. Just the thing. Lose himself up in the park for a week, or two weeks, whatever. Susie could keep in touch with Josie. A little odd, maybe, but old folks are a little odd.

"Well, we'll see. The boys are so anxious to see you and go fishing and all. Say, could you possibly take them on your trip?"

Ranse laughed his booming laugh. "No chance. Maybe if I was going alone. But this guy I'm taking is a dedicated fisherman who hates kids."

"Oh, all right. We'll probably come up anyway. Any word from Mother?"

"Just a letter yesterday. Nothing new. She's still holding the fort out there."

"Okay, Dad. Have a good fishing trip. Good-bye."

When Ranse put down the phone, he began to whistle and then to sing, and then he let out a shout that echoed through the empty house. Rule Three: improvise. That was the thing. Think fast. He went to the closet and brought out his sleeping bag–still in good shape–then to the garage. From the boards along the ceiling rafters, he brought down his small, one-man tent, rolled neatly in its duffel bag. Got his tackle box out from the locked cupboard and checked it over. Everything in order. He'd leave tomorrow early. Put the canoe on top of the car, buy his supplies at the store near the entrance to the park, and just plain disappear for as long as was needed. Oh yes, make a couple of phone calls to tell people where he was going, like to the postmaster to have him hold the mail.

The perfect solution!

It was just about noon. He had the rest of the day to get ready. He went back into the house, and as he climbed the steps he heard the phone again. That would be Josie. Well, if the twins weren't born, she'd stay until they were; if they were born, she'd be needed for at least a couple of weeks. He could call her from time to time from the booths in the park.

He picked up the phone.

"Hello. Mr. McGruber?"

My God, it was her! His voice caught in his throat.
"Yeah."

"This is Madelaine–from the bank."

"Madelaine. Oh, yeah. Sure. How are you?"

"I'm fine, Mr. McGruber. I was wondering. Well, just say no if you want to. But it's such a hot day, I was wondering if my boy friend and I could come out after work and swim?"

Boy friend? Of course she would have a boy friend. Or perhaps she didn't. "Yeah, that would be fine. Sure."

"Oh, thanks. We won't be any bother, and we do want to swim. We'll be out about five."

"Fine. If I'm not here, just go ahead and have your swim."

"Oh."

Was there disappointment in her voice? "But I'll probably be here."

"Super. See you then."

Now, why in the world hadn't he put this girl off as he had his daughter? Because she wasn't his daughter? He felt a stirring in his groin as he thought of her. Her white skin and dark hair and red lips. Those red, inviting lips. Well, with her boy friend along, she wouldn't have eyes for a sixty-year-old, even if the sixty-year-old did have a flat stomach and hair on his chest.

Who the hell was he kidding? A boy friend would be young, athletic, full of hormones. Besides, why was she coming now? Was there any connection between this and the robbery? He was suspicious of the boy friend. He was suspicious of everybody.

CHAPTER NINE

It was hot, terribly hot for the first half of August. As five o'clock approached, Ranse, who'd been restless all afternoon, found himself becoming agitated. He sat on the porch and watched the parking space below him, and, sure enough, at almost exactly five o'clock a powder blue Datsun pulled in and stopped.

Ranse stayed where he was. The door of the car opened, and Madelaine got out. She was wearing a sort of loose thing, also blue, that seemed to be made of towelling.

"Hello, up there," she shouted.

Ranse got up and went to meet her.

"Where's the boy friend?" he asked.

"Couldn't come." She pushed her hair off her face and smiled up at him. A smile that was soft and inviting? "Do you mind?"

"No, no, of course not."

"Will you come swimming with me? Know what they say: never swim alone."

"Sure will!" Ranse felt gay and carefree and at least forty years younger. He wasn't thinking, he was merely reacting, reacting in a way that any male would react when invited by a beautiful girl to go swimming.

"You go on down to the beach. I'll get my trunks on."

In his bedroom, as he squeezed into his bathing trunks, he admonished himself. "You behave yourself now, or there won't be room for you in these things."

When he got to the beach, she was sitting on the dock in a deck chair. She was wearing a polka dot bikini, the bra of which scarcely contained her beautiful white breasts. Her long legs were crossed and one dainty foot was slowly moving up and down.

As he looked at her, Ranse was reminded of another girl he had known thirty-five years before. A girl he'd never seen since, but who had never been completely out of his mind. Often she came to him in dreams, always young, always beautiful, always free and uninhibited.

She was a Wren stationed at H.M.C.S. *York*, and the commanding officer had suggested that Ranse interview her.

"What's the problem?" Ranse had asked.

"I don't know exactly." The C.O. was a Maritimer, a lean, silent man who ran the ship with as little fuss as possible, delegating authority to his officers. "I keep hearing these stories–or hints. Innuendoes. I wish you'd check it out."

"Check out what about whom, sir?"

"This Wren, Petree. Works in the paymaster's office. You may have noticed her. Really magnificent figure."

"That's a crime in the navy?"

"No, of course not. But it seems she's pretty free with her favours. Well, not exactly free. A disturbing influence among the ratings. And I keep getting scuttlebutt about a lottery."

"You mean she's selling tickets?"

"Something like that. Better check it out."

So Lieutenant McGruber, Provost Officer, had called Wren Petree into his office. She did indeed have a magnificent figure. And something more. A great deal more. There was an aura of sexiness about her, in her gestures, her walk, the tilt of her head, but, most of all, in the way she used her face. Everything about her was exciting, made a man want to forget everything else and get her into bed. Helen of Troy and Cleopatra must have had just such an aura.

She stood in front of Lieutenant McGruber's desk, saluted and smiled.

"You wanted to see me, sir?"

"Ah, yes. Sit down please, Petree. Smoke if you want to."

"I don't smoke, sir. It ruins your breath."

"Yes, yes, of course. Well, you won't mind if I do?" He lit a cigarette and wondered just what one could say to a girl who was suspected of auctioning her favours.

"Ah, Petree. How long have you been in the service?"

"Six months, sir, and ten days."

"Do you like it?"

"Oh yes, sir. Very much."

"Why?"

"Well, I like this uniform and, well"–she smiled her disarming smile–"what woman wouldn't like being surrounded by so many neat men?"

"You think they are neat?"

"Gorgeous."

This was going a bit too fast for Lieutenant McGruber. "Where is your home, Petree?"

"Toronto. I was born right here. Down in the Beaches area."

"Um, hmm." He thumbed through her file. "Senior Matric, I see, along with typing and bookkeeping."

"Yes, sir. Lieutenant Habor says I'm the fastest typist and the best he's ever had." It was stated as a matter of fact. A rather dull fact, but one that needed stating. "Has he complained about my work, sir?" She was looking at him with disarming interest.

"No, no, nothing like that."

"Whew, I'm glad of that."

"Then why are you here, eh? Well, it's something quite different."

"I've been very careful not to break any navy rules."

"I'm not sure you have. At least I've never seen a regulation against it. Tell me, you said you liked the men here. Do you date any of them?"

She smiled at him indulgently. "What do you think, sir?"

"Yes, yes, of course. Natural thing to do. Any particular one?"

"Sometimes."

Oh, hell, he might as well come out with it. "Petree, there's some scuttlebutt around the ship about a lottery?"

She smiled openly. "You mean like the football pools and like that?"

"Not exactly. There's talk about a draw in the Leading Seamen's mess. Very special tickets and the winner receives a most unusual prize."

"A good prize?" she asked, and again that half curious, half exploratory look.

"I think so. It's rumoured that the winner gets to spend the night with the most desirable Wren on the ship."

There was just enough of a pause. "I can't think who that would be, sir."

Suddenly Ranse saw his way out of his predicament. "I see. Well, if you find out, or even if you don't, you might pass the word that the C.O. is aware of what is going on and wants it to stop. Let it be known that it could mean a bad discharge for the person involved. A charge of immorality is serious in the navy. Will you do that?"

"Yes, sir, I will." Her inviting, frank, fun-loving, brown eyes were smiling into his, promising delights such as he'd never known. "And thank you, sir."

"Yes. Well, that's all, Petree. You can go now."

But she didn't get up. "You didn't ask me where I live, sir." She reached over to his desk pad, tore off the top sheet, wrote something on it, and slid it towards him. "This is my address. Perhaps you'd like to drop in for a cup of tea. This evening?"

"Well."

She leaned ever so slightly towards him, young breasts bulging her uniform, lips slightly moist. "I'd like to show you my gratitude."

Then she stood up straight at attention. Ranse stood, too. She saluted smartly, turned, and walked out of the office. Ranse watched her delectable bottom until it was gone.

He picked up the paper. Her address was there, written

in a neat hand, and, below it, her telephone number. Just such a slip of paper, he knew, was residing in the pockets of a number of eager ratings. He knew also there would be no further draws in the Leading Seamen's mess and that each disappointed rating would get his dollar back.

He knew something else. Nothing on earth would keep him from making that phone call and going around for that cup of tea. He did, and it was all that he could have anticipated and more. It was strictly a one-night affair. His recommendation to the C.O. was that she be drafted out to Halifax, forthwith, which she was. Ranse never heard from her again, but there'd been scarcely a day or night in the years since that he hadn't had at least a fleeting thought of Wren Petree.

And now this girl, wearing a skin-tight bikini and dangling a shapely bare leg, was smiling at him in that same easy, natural way that Wren Petree had done.

"I hope you don't mind my coming out alone," she said. "It's so hot in town. So many people and cars and gas fumes. And here . . . ." She stretched her arms above her head and Ranse nearly burst his shorts. "It's so quiet and peaceful and cool. I don't care if I don't go swimming."

Ranse didn't know what to say. If only she'd stop looking at him in that way! "The water's nice," he said lamely.

"I'm glad Willie couldn't come," she said without guile.

"Willie? Do I know him?"

"Probably not. He's new in town. Hasn't a job yet, as far as I know. At least, he doesn't cash any pay cheques."

Ranse laughed. "Can't keep much from our friendly local bank. Does he come in often?"

"Not really. He opened a chequing account. With cash."

"Does that happen often?"

"No. Hardly ever. But it's easier that way for strangers. Otherwise, we have to investigate the cheque and get identification."

"Would the bank ask questions? I mean if it were a large amount of cash?"

"No. Why should we?" She smiled at him knowingly. He wondered.

"Were you in the bank when it was robbed?"

"Was I ever. I'll never forget it."

"Did you notice anything? In particular, I mean?" Why was he asking these damned questions?

She smiled again. "No more than anyone else, I guess. He was disguised you know. And we were on our faces before we realized what was happening."

"Were you frightened?"

"Not really. Somehow I had a feeling he wouldn't hurt us. Why do you ask?"

"Oh, just a detective's habit of asking questions. Do you think it could have been . . . ."

"Willie? Good Lord, no. I mean, I don't think so." She was thinking. "But then he was disguised. It really could have been anyone. Except you. He didn't have a beard."

She was very close to him. Ranse moved back. "Look, if you don't want to swim, we could go up to the patio. I'll buy you a drink."

"Oh?"

"I think I need one, too. And it's more–" He stopped.

"Private up there?"

"Matter of fact it is. I've kept enough trees between the house and the lake."

She turned and, before he realized what was happening, dived off the dock. He could see her slim, bronzed body shimmering under the water. When she came up, about twenty feet away, she was facing him, and one delicious breast had escaped from its confinement. Through the clear water he could see it, bulging, shimmering. She made no move to imprison it.

"The water's lovely," she called. "Come on in."

Ranse walked to the end of the dock, and was about to plunge in when he remembered his false beard.

"Oh, oh, almost forgot. For some reason, this time of year, water gives me hay fever."

"Must be the pollen," she said, doing a gentle breast

stroke towards the dock. She was right below him now and he was looking down at her smiling, beaded face, the naughty breast still loose. She held one hand up to him and he reached down and took it. She placed a foot on the end of the dock, and he gently pulled her out of the water, the wayward breast coming dangerously close to his face as she came up. For a moment, she stood facing him, wet face six inches from his own, waiting. Then she said, "Towel, please."

He handed her her towel and looked away. When he looked back, the breast was back in place. She didn't say anything silly like, "Show's over," or indicate any embarrassment or coquetry. Girls like her don't need tricks, he thought. Their presence is enough.

"Now," she said, "I really would like a long, cool drink."

Ranse led the way along the short, winding path through the oaks and birches to the patio. He moved the wrought-iron arm chair close to the round table.

"Sit while I fix us a drink."

When he came out to the patio with two tall gin and tonics and a newly opened can of nuts, she was leaning back with eyes closed. She opened them and smiled.

"Such a wonderful place, trees and solitude. It must be fun to be retired."

"Not all it's cracked up to be."

"Oh?"

"Sure." He sat down close beside her on the padded chaise longue and sipped his drink. "Everybody thinks that retirement will be wonderful. Nothing to do but sit in the sun and fish and putter about. Gets terribly boring."

"Oh, I'd love it!" She sipped her drink and smiled her satisfaction with it.

"I'd trade it all to be your age again."

"Thirty? Not all it's cracked up to be, either."

He started to fish. "When I was thirty I'd been married five years and had two kids."

She laughed. "And your next question might be: why aren't I?"

"Oh, I know all about women's lib. And I think I understand some of it. But it seems such a waste."

"Of what? These breasts that you find so enchanting? They should be suckling babies?"

He couldn't help but blush. And she laughed at his discomfiture. Then she took another sip of her drink and turned serious.

"You're right, of course. These brief affairs are so unsatisfying–and really not much fun."

"Really? I should think they'd be a lot of fun. Don't you like men?"

Again the tinkling laugh. "Oh, you. No, no, I'm not a lesbian, if that's what you're thinking. It's just that, well, I loved my father."

"Natural enough. At least I think so, despite all this guff about kids hating their parents."

"No. I mean I was in love with my father."

Stillness now. A cicada buzzed from a treetop and a chipmunk chirped from the undergrowth. Ranse looked up into a birch, not to find the cicada, but to avoid her glance.

"I think I'm going to tell you something that I've never told anyone."

No answer.

She continued. "From the time I was a tiny girl, my father and I were pals. I loved him so. He taught me to swim and ride a bike and fish. I'm a good fisherman, you know."

Still no answer. Ranse was afraid of what was coming. He wanted to stop her, but he couldn't.

"We were the greatest of pals. You see, my mother, well, she and Daddy never did get along. She nagged him."

Still no comment.

"I was fifteen when she died, and, well, fully developed. And, from being pals, my father and I became lovers."

"The son of a bitch!" It was hardly audible, but she heard it.

Everything in Ranse's life and code and moral sense

was affronted. He'd encountered it, of course, when he was on the vice squad. Down around Parliament Street and Jarvis, the lower depths of Toronto in the late thirties and forties. He'd encountered it. Young girls raped by their fathers, or uncles, or friends of the family, who almost invariably ended up as prostitutes.

She came to him and laid a soft hand on his bare shoulder. "Please, you mustn't blame Daddy. It was I who seduced him. And it wasn't nasty or rotten; it was beautiful."

"A kid of fifteen!"

"A woman. We loved each other truly. He was such a kind, loving, gentle man. And I miss him so much." She was crying now, softly and silently.

"He's dead?"

"Ten years ago. And since then I've known the usual number of men, some who made love to me, some who wanted to marry me. But none as kind and loving and gentle as Daddy."

Ranse took her small, soft hand in his big, hard one.

"You see, I'm spoiled. I think maybe I've been searching for a man, like my father, who would hold me and cuddle me and love me and not make demands on me." Slowly, she slipped down onto his lap, where he sat stretched out on the longue. Her soft, warm, almost naked body. "Please be kind to me," she whispered.

His arms closed around her, and he stood up with her still in his arms, so light and fragile. Then he carried her into the house and to the soft, big bed.

When Ranse opened his eyes, it was dark, and for a moment he couldn't remember what had happened. Then he remembered and felt for his beard. It was in place, evidently undisturbed. He felt the other side of the bed, but it was empty. There were no lights anywhere in the house. Softly he called her name, but knew there would be no answer. Then he reached for the bed lamp and switched it on. He got out of bed, naked, and walked to the kitchen and turned on that light.

Propped up against the toaster was a note, written with a felt pen on list paper. He picked it up and read:

"Don't you ever kiss a girl when you make love? I know prostitutes don't like to be kissed, but, really, I'm not one. Or were you afraid I'd chew your beard?"

Ranse's stomach hit rock bottom. What did she mean by that? Had she discovered his beard was false? Damn! How could he have let this happen? He picked up the list pad and threw it across the room. Damn! Damn! Damn! Everything had worked until now. Now if this little bitch guessed something and the finger of suspicion was pointed at him. . . . God!

Prostitute, eh? Well, that's what she was, all right. And that story about her father. Probably a pack of lies. And he'd fallen for it. Just like any teenager with a hot crotch. Lost control of himself. Forgot all precaution. Women. They could do that to him every time!

And then he remembered the warmth of her, the softness of her, the beautiful feel of her, and he relented. If she were there now, he knew he'd do it all again. Oh God, the thought of it!

His mind reverted to the practical. She either guessed or she didn't. The thing to do was follow his original plan and go fishing. But first a rasher of bacon and eggs. God he was hungry.

The next morning at first light he loaded the canoe onto the roof rack of his car, stowed his fishing gear, tent, sleeping bag, and cooking utensils into the trunk and headed north.

At the first town he came to, he found a phone booth and phoned Josie collect. No, nothing had happened. Yes, Helen was fine. Yes, she wanted to stay as long as she was needed, but she missed him terribly.

"And I miss you, too. I'm off fishing now into the park, but I'll phone a couple of times from the ranger station to check how things are. Yes, I'll be careful. Likewise. Take care of yourself, and give my love to everybody."

He hung up and headed for the wilderness park and solitude.

CHAPTER TEN

September fourth.

Ranse McGruber stood in front of the bathroom mirror, fingering his new beard. Didn't look much different from the old one. Little shorter, but then, he could say, he'd had to trim it down because the deer flies kept getting into it. Deer flies are an awful nuisance to beards. Most important, it was his own. The false beard, the one that had cost him over a hundred dollars, was gone. Completely. One of the first things he'd done when he got to Portage Lake and was sitting alone by his campfire on the shore, was to hold it over the fire on a stick, like a kid roasting a wiener, and hear it sizzle and sputter and watch it disappear. Last bit of evidence gone.

The trip had done him good in other ways. He was tanned and hard. The muscles on his arms and shoulders were firm from paddling and climbing and carrying his canoe over rocky trails. Stomach flat, leg muscles strong, and he hadn't had a drink in almost a month. The outdoor life, a diet of fresh fish and canned beans, mostly. It had made a new man of him.

A new man. He most surely was. A criminal. Nothing could ever change that. But only if he got caught. A man is innocent until proven guilty: this was the bulwark of British justice. And no one now could ever prove him guilty, or even suspect him.

Except maybe one person.

And he was rich. More than two hundred thousand

dollars sitting there waiting for him. Invested in savings certificates at thirteen and a half per cent meant, let's see, over twenty-seven thousand a year without touching the principal. If he bought the right stocks, it would earn even more than that, maybe twice as much. My God, he'd lost almost two thousand dollars already by letting it sit there without drawing interest.

If it was still there. Maybe somebody had found it! No, impossible. And the old problem returned to his mind. How to get it? How to use it? Were the serial numbers of the bills known? That was the remaining evidence against him–the money. The money, which he'd thought would solve all his problems, could create the biggest problem.

Tomorrow he'd drive to Toronto airport and pick up Josie. She'd told him when he'd phoned her last, "Ranse, darling, we've got two more beautiful grandchildren! Twins! One of each. Oh, they're lovely!" There was more, much more. She'd made reservations for the fifth.

First things first. Drive to town and pick up his mail. Do some banking. Get some groceries, and some booze.

In the post office, his box was jammed full of magazines, newspapers, circulars, bills, and letters. A card told him there was more waiting for him at the desk.

"Where'd you go, Ranse?" the postmaster asked, as he lifted a bundle from the box behind him, a bundle of mail tied with a string, and set it on the counter in front of Ranse.

"Up in the park. Found a little lake near the north end, where I've never been before. Took a lot of paddling and portaging to get there, but it was worth it."

"Fishing good?"

"Great. More than I could eat. Put most of them back."

"Ah, you're lucky. Nothing to do but fish."

"What's new in town?"

"Pretty quiet since the robbery."

"Did they catch the guy? I didn't even have a radio up there."

"Well, Joe Who is still prime minister. And our bountiful government is about to give the Chrysler Corporation a big bundle of money. No, they haven't seen hide nor hair of the guy who robbed the bank. They'll never see any of that money again."

"Oh?"

"Hear the bank didn't have the serial numbers of any of the bills. Most of it came in that day. Crook sure knew when the bank'd be full of money."

"Usually do." Ranse was going through the bundle of mail. He extracted his pension cheques. Next stop, the bank.

The bank was crowded, with a lineup in front of each wicket. Probably the last time it would be so crowded this year. Just inside the door, a young OPP officer stood with arms folded, watching the customers. Shutting the barn door after the horse is gone, Ranse thought.

Ranse made out his deposit slip and joined the line at Madelaine's wicket. He was upset to realize that his heart was pounding and he was somewhat tongue-tied.

When he reached the head of the line she gave him her best bank-teller smile.

"Good morning, Mr. McGruber. We haven't seen you in some time."

"Been away. Fishing."

She took his cheques and deposit slip and stamped them professionally. "Catch anything?"

He leaned towards her. "Look, I'm sorry about what happened. I'd like to explain. Maybe you'd like a swim after work."

"Thank you," she said. "You're looking very well. I like the way you've trimmed your beard. Most becoming." She counted out his cash, and he knew it was time to go. He put the money into his wallet and left the wicket. "Good morning, Mrs. Graham," he heard her saying to the next customer, with, he knew, the same smile she'd given him. "And how are you this morning?"

Ranse didn't hear the answer. He didn't want to. He went back out to the street.

He made a quick trip down to the liquor store, then back to the main street and the supermarket. There he picked up some fresh tomatoes at $1.69 a pound and bought some bananas at 29¢ a pound. The tomatoes, he knew, came from less than a hundred miles away and the bananas from several thousand. Everything else he bought had gone up about five per cent in the short time he'd been away. But Ranse didn't care. He was a rich man.

As he drove up the main street, he pulled in front of the Community Hall to see what was playing. It was Bernard Slade's *Same Time, Next Year*, and the billboard said in homemade lettering, "A rollicking modern comedy about adultery." Yeah, adultery is rollicking, all right. Yeah!

Back home in the quiet of his own woods, Ranse went about the chores of getting his canoe back into the water and stowing his camping gear in the cupboards of the garage. He could scarcely find the crack where he'd hidden the key. And all the time he thought of Madelaine, just as he'd thought of her almost every waking hour since he'd made love to her. A rollicking comedy about adultery. It was easy. All you had to do was, well, do it. Nothing more natural in this world.

When he was a youth, plays about adulterous adventures tended to end tragically. Since the adulterors broke God's law, they had to suffer, suffer, suffer. Now plays on the same subject were rollicking comedies. And in this good, solid, religious community, nobody so much as lifted an eyebrow. Maybe he'd go and see the play tonight.

It was hot for September, and he wondered if Madelaine would wear her bikini. If she came at all. As five o'clock drew near, he found himself pacing the floor and glancing down at the driveway. Surely she would come. There was unfinished business.

And she did. Shortly after five, a low-slung sports car roared along his winding driveway and came to a grinding stop. It looked to Ranse like a Porsche. A lean, blonde young man leaped out of the driver's seat without opening the door, and lifted Madelaine out after him. They were both laughing happily and both dressed in T-shirts and very tight jeans.

As they came towards the patio, Ranse studied the young man with interest. A type new to him–open-faced, self-confident, natural. But Ranse's professional eye detected a wariness, a watchfulness. He decided he didn't like this young man.

"Ranse," Madelaine said, with a smile very much like her bank-teller smile. "I want you to meet Willie Schmitt. Willie, Ranse McGruber."

"Please call me Willie." He pronounced it *Villie*.

"Okay. Uh, have a seat. It's nice out here on the patio. What can I get you to drink?"

"Beer would be nice," Willie said.

"Just a Coke," Madelaine said.

Ranse said, "I think I need a double scotch." He glanced at Madelaine, but her expression was still impersonal and aloof.

When he came out with the drinks, they were talking quietly together, but stopped when he came near.

"Well, uh, Willie," Ranse said, handing them the glasses, "have you been in this country long?"

"I am here just over six months. *Ja.*"

"And what brings you to this neck of the woods?"

A puzzled frown. "To this neck . . . ?"

"He means here, to this area," Madelaine explained, placing a hand on his.

"Oh, I see. Well, I think maybe I can get some work here. Maybe some building."

"Willie is a carpenter. He's thinking of starting a small contracting business, if he can get some capital."

"I see. Well, good luck." Ranse took a long pull of his drink. It felt good.

"Thank you." The young man was holding his bottle of beer in front of his face, gazing speculatively at Ranse over it. "I like your beard," he said.

"Well, thanks. It . . . ." But Ranse could think of nothing more to add.

"I've thought of growing a beard, too. Maybe make me

101

look younger. A good disguise, *ja?*" He laughed loudly at this, and Madelaine laughed, too. Ranse really didn't consider it funny.

To change the subject, Ranse asked, "Where is home for you?"

"Home?"

"I mean before you came to Ontario and to Muskoka."

A slight veil of caution closed over the young man's eyes. Ranse had seen this many times if, when talking to youths, a question came close to something that needed concealment. This young man, he decided, would bear watching. He was no fool, that was certain. And how did he happen to be here, now, with Madelaine? Chance? She had said she was uninterested in young men, had, in fact, convinced him of that; but maybe he'd just wanted to be convinced.

"I came from East Germany," the young Adonis said. "I am what you call–"

"A defector," Madelaine prompted.

"Yes, that is right. I am a swimmer. We were at a meet in Montreal. I, as you say, ran away." He grinned broadly. "Oh, don't worry, your government knows all about me. I have a permit to stay."

"You didn't like it in East Germany?"

The young man grimaced. "You wouldn't believe what it is like, if I told you."

Well, you certainly got enough to eat, anyway, Ranse thought, looking at the muscular arms and legs and flat stomach. Another refugee. How gullible we are, he thought. Anyone who comes from a Communist country and says he's a refugee, we welcome with open arms. Just tell us how bad things are there, bad-mouth your own country, tell us about your great yearning for freedom, and we believe you and give you the freedom of the country. How many fifth columnists are getting into our country by this means? he wondered. Precisely the way the Nazis had managed to take over Norway and other countries during the war. Work from within.

He sipped his drink. What the hell? Probably the young

man was telling the truth. The policeman's habit of not believing anyone never dies. And what about him, Ranse? Could anyone believe him any more? He'd deceived his friends, and his wife, and his family. From now on he must always be on guard. Never allow a careless moment, never get drunk and talkative, and dare not even talk in his sleep.

He looked at the young woman sitting across from him, and his hormones acted up. Had she deceived him? Was she lying to him all the time? How did it come about that she'd suddenly got the urge to swim on his beach? And he had fallen for it. And, by God, he would fall for it again, given the chance. He wondered if he would ever get that chance.

The young man was finishing his beer and looking about him. "I think this is the best place I find yet. These lakes and trees and rocks–perfect."

"It changes some in winter," Ranse remarked.

"Yes, I hear you have lots of snow and the skiing is good. Next to swimming, I love to ski. Maybe I can get a job to, what you say, *unterrichten*."

"Instruct," Madelaine prompted.

Now, how did she come to know German? he wondered. Good Lord, he was getting suspicious of everything.

"*Ja.* The instructor. In Germany, I was member of ski patrol and . . . ." He stopped, and again the veil of caution narrowed his eyes, oh so slightly. "Mostly I want to be a good Canadian citizen."

Lies, Ranse thought, all lies. "You speak English very well for having been here such a short time," he said to the young man.

"*Ja*, we learn it in school. English is one of our most important subjects. Everybody must know English."

"Why is that?"

"The universal language. Everywhere people speak English. Here, in the United States, England, even in Russia. Everywhere. Somebody speaks English wherever you go."

"Makes sense."

"And what do you do, sir?"

Sir? What the hell was with this sir? Make him feel old, that's what. How much had Madelaine told him?

"Do?" he asked.

"*Ja.* You are young man still. You must do something."

"Well, I'm sort of retired."

"Ranse was chief of detectives in Toronto," Madelaine explained.

Again the wary look. "Detective. Must be interesting work."

"Very. But I'm out of it now. Just taking it easy until I find something I want to do. Perhaps I, too, will become a carpenter."

"Maybe we go in business together." He said it, but obviously didn't mean it.

"Well, is anyone going to swim?" Ranse asked.

"I like that very much." The young man stood up and peeled off his tight jeans. Underneath was a very brief pair of swim trunks, such as Ranse had seen on television worn by contestants in the swimming meets. They bulged significantly in the crotch. His legs were hard as steel.

"I'll come too," Madelaine said, and removed her own jeans. Ranse left his clothing on. They went to the edge of the dock and Willie dived in, using the prescribed racers' dive, and struck out with powerful strokes. Soon he was a hundred yards out into the lake.

"Why did you bring him along?" Ranse asked Madelaine, who was still standing beside him, too close for comfort.

"Isn't he something?" she said.

"Yeah, something. Magnificent swimmer."

"That's not all he does magnificently."

Ranse felt a twinge of jealousy. He moved closer to her and put his arm around her bare shoulder. "That kiss we missed the other night. I'm ready to make payment in full."

"I'll just bet you are. But not out here, in plain view of everyone. What would the neighbours say?"

"All gone home."

"You never can tell. Mustn't have people telling tales to your wife. You're in enough trouble already."

"Me? Trouble? What do you mean?"

She lifted a long, lean finger and stroked his beard. "I think I liked it better when it was . . . longer."

Damn. Why had she said that? What had she noticed when they were making love? He'd gone right to sleep afterwards. But had she?

Willie was coming back, using a powerful breast stroke, blonde head ducking and reappearing rhythmically. He stopped and waved. "Come on in. Are you the chicken?"

Madelaine laughed and plunged in, swimming out to where he was treading water. As she approached, he swam towards her and embraced her in the water, lifting her high in the air and kissing her as she came down hard against him.

That was too much for Ranse. He turned and walked back to the patio, slumped into a chair and finished his scotch. What in hell was wrong with him? he wondered. What had happened? In just over a month he had changed completely, forgotten about his wife and gone panting after an enticing little bit in a bikini. It had a horrible sense of déjà vu. Sixty-year-old and his secretary, or some call girl he'd picked up, embezzling from the firm and running off. Never underestimate the power of long, smooth limbs and soft willing lips and . . . . Oh, God! Now it was happening to him. A girl younger than his daughters, and he wanted her. God, how he wanted her. Every muscle in his body ached for her. He could, he knew, steal for her, kill for her.

He got up and poured himself another drink. As he sat down, he could hear their laughter and banter from the water. He knocked off his drink in one mighty gulp.

CHAPTER ELEVEN

"Well?" Madelaine asked.

The Porsche was tearing along Muskoka 75 at over one hundred kilometres an hour. The road was narrow and winding. No shoulders: in some places the granite and trees came right down to the road; in others deep ditches ran on either side. The turns were tight and murderous, accounting for the speed limit of 60 km/h posted along the sides. But Willie ignored the signs, taking the turns with the skill of a professional race driver, his entire concentration on his driving.

"Well what?" he asked.

"What do you think of my friend Ranse?"

"I think he is in love with you."

"Infatuated, you mean."

"No difference. He wants to put his arms about you and make love to you, hard and often."

"That's not what I mean," she answered with some irritation. "What do you think about my theory?"

"Your theory. What can you say? You thought his beard was loose when he was making love to you. You had been drinking. What can you say? 'This man is guilty. I discover it when I am making love to him. No, I have no witnesses to this love making. No, I can't be sure his beard was loose.' His beard now is certainly not false. Who will believe you?"

"Perhaps he will."

"Oh, ho. So you think we can blackmail him, *ja*?"

"Perhaps."

"Blackmail is a dangerous thing–very dangerous. Besides, we would have no hope. He would laugh at us, unless we had more evidence."

"Well then, we must get it."

"Yes, maybe. But how?"

She fell silent then, thinking about Ranse and her theory. "He said he was driving to Toronto tomorrow. He'll be away all day. Perhaps you could pay him a little visit."

At Highway 200, which led into town, they came to a stop sign. He applied the brakes and the Porsche came to a grinding stop in a shower of dust and stones. He shifted into low and was about to turn onto the highway when a horn blew behind him. Madelaine looked back.

"My God," she gasped, "it's the OPP!"

"The police? I mustn't let them catch me!" He began to release the clutch.

"No no, you mustn't. You could never get away from them. They'll have your licence number. It's not serious."

Willie put the car into neutral and pulled on the emergency brake.

The officer got out of his car and came up beside Willie.

"May I see your driver's licence, please?" he asked politely.

Willie smiled at him. "What is wrong, officer?"

"I've been following you for a couple of miles. The speed you were going, if you'd met another car, you'd have been in big trouble."

"But there were no other cars."

"Your licence, please."

"But, officer, surely–"

"Give him the licence!" Madelaine hissed in his ear.

Willie smiled again, fished into the tight rear pocket of his jeans and pulled out his wallet. He flipped over the cards until he came to the one with his licence, and held it up towards the policeman.

"Take it out, please," the officer requested.

Willie shrugged, extracted the licence from its celluloid envelope and handed it to the policeman.

The officer took it, copied down the information into his notebook. "I clocked you at a hundred in a sixty zone," he said. "I'll have to give you a ticket."

"But, officer."

"Yes?"

"I am new in the country. I don't know yet all the rules."

"I assume you can read English."

"Yes, of course."

"Well, the laws apply to you as well as anyone else. Your penalty is fifty dollars. You can mail it in, or you can appear in court in Barrie and defend the case."

Willie shrugged and took the ticket. Then, as the policeman walked back to his patrol car, he shifted into gear and turned onto the highway.

"Damn!" he said. "This is bad!"

"It's only a fine for speeding. Everybody gets them. I'll help you pay it," Madelaine reassured him.

"It is more than that."

"Why?"

Suddenly he smiled. "You are right. Only a fine for speeding. I will mail it in. Nobody needs to know anything about it." In the rear-view mirror he noted the patrol car had turned in the opposite direction on the highway. He shifted gears and took the next curve at one hundred and twenty.

When they reached the little house that Madelaine and a friend rented on a secluded spot on the lakeshore, Willie wheeled the Porsche into the narrow driveway and came to an abrupt but smooth stop. Madelaine was flushed and excited.

"I never saw anyone drive like that," she gasped.

"It is easy in such a car. It is tested so many times in Germany, not only on the Autobahn, but on the winding mountain roads. You see, the suspension–"

"Please. Not a lecture on sports cars. I know nothing about them and wouldn't understand."

108

"Bah! Women."

"Would you like to come in?" She kept her voice even, but her pulse was racing. The excitement of the ride and the nearness of the muscular bare torso had done it.

"What about your roommate?"

"Sailing with her boy friend. I have a strong feeling she won't be back until morning."

"I see. Yes, I think I would like to come in–very much."

Later, as she lay on her back beside him, smoking a cigarette, Madelaine felt contented and happy. And contemplative. This, she realized, was what she really had been waiting for. Not old men who go to sleep and snore after one encounter. Not one of the local beer-drinking, truck-driving swains, who slapped her ass and told her she had great boobs. But a young man, hard and lean, with finesse and skill, who was ready when she was, and could prolong the experience excruciatingly.

And a man who needed money. She'd had a peek at his bank balance and knew it was meagre. Oh, yes, he needed money. The payments on the Porsche, she also knew, were a little overdue. Here was a man who was ready for adventure and intrigue, as she herself was ready.

She ran her fingers delicately over his almost hairless chest and let them dance southward. My God, he was ready again!

Later, sitting at the small round table by the window, drinking a liqueur, she laid her hand lightly on his bare shoulder.

He smiled. "There are limits, you know."

She laughed. "I doubt that. But I want to talk."

A slight frown crossed his brow. "Seriously?"

"Yes, seriously."

"You know all there is to know about me. I came to Montreal . . . ."

"No. Something else. What we were discussing in the car."

"Oh, yes. Your friend the bank robber."

"He is! I'm sure of it!"

"And you want to send him to jail. Was he that bad?"

"No. Listen, Willie, I don't want to send him to jail. But we can get that money!"

"And how are we to get it, this money that we don't know he has? And we have no evidence except your feelings about the beard."

"It's more than just the beard."

"*Ja?*"

"In the bank. The robber. The way he looked at me just for a second. A man can disguise everything but his eyes."

"We still need the evidence."

"Then we must get the evidence."

He shook his head.

"Oh, Willie, can't you see? This is our chance to get rich. Over two hundred thousand dollars! Invested properly, it could set us up for life. We could get away from here, far away. To the Caribbean!"

"Caribbean?"

"There are hundreds of islands. And the swimming and diving are marvellous."

"But no skiing."

"We could go to Switzerland for skiing. We could do whatever we wanted. And we could be together."

"Yes, that would be nice."

"Did you like me, Willie?"

"I like you very much. You are like a European girl."

"Oh, Willie, think of it. Enough money to do what we wanted. No more working in that stuffy bank, smiling at customers I hate. 'Yes, Mrs. Winninger. Thank you, Mr. Bourling.' "

"I see. And you think the money would take you away from it all. Wouldn't it be easier to just, what you say, *unterschlagen?*"

"What?"

"You know, take a little here or there."

"Embezzle?"

"*Ja.*"

"No. Impossible. People do it, but they get caught sooner or later. This will be better."

Willie threw back his head and laughed. "Better to steal from a cunning man who may have some money and who may not?"

"I'm sure he has it hidden somewhere. I'm sure of it. He did go away for a while and might have taken the money somewhere else. But I just have a feeling! If we could find it and take it–don't you see?–he couldn't go to the police."

"And how are we to find this money?"

She leaned towards him conspiratorily. "You must go to his place. He said that tomorrow he would be driving to the airport to meet his wife. There will be nobody there all day."

"And I am to go there and search?"

"Yes, yes. It will be easy. You can't see his place from the road."

"And if somebody sees my car on the road, or sees me pull into his driveway?"

"I've thought of that, too."

"You've been busy thinking."

"Listen. Don't drive your car into his driveway."

"You mean walk?"

"No, swim. Listen." She was excited. "There are no cottages from Ranse's place for almost a mile around the lake. It's been zoned as open land. And there is an old road down to one of the points. Nobody uses it, except on weekends, and not even then at this time of year. He told me about it. You could park on this road and swim from the point around to Ranse's place. There is plenty of cover in the woods. Nobody would notice you."

"I see."

"If you go early in the morning, you could spend the whole day at his place, looking."

"Yes, that is true."

"Think, Willie. The money must be there somewhere. Hidden in the house, or somewhere on the lot. Perhaps in the garage, or under a loose patio stone."

He was looking at her speculatively. "You are *quite* something. What if I don't find anything?"

"Then we must keep trying. Listen, from the same

point you can see Ranse's place. You could hide among the rocks and trees and watch him with binoculars. Sooner or later, he would give himself away."

"A lot of work."

"But it's worth it. Don't you see? It's worth it!"

"Vell, maybe." He stood up and effortlessly lifted her from her chair and held her against him. "But right now there is another project. *Ja.*"

CHAPTER TWELVE

When her son-in-law had driven her to the airport in Regina, Josie McGruber had thought how nice it was to be going home. She'd missed her husband terribly. "Never marry a cop," her best friend had warned her, but Josie couldn't have helped herself if she'd wanted to. And she had never regretted it. For Josie had married for love, and Josie believed in love. Terms like "falling head over heels" and "being struck dumb" she took literally. She still went about her work humming or softly singing love songs: "You do something to me, something that simply mystifies me." And although there had been bad times, times when she felt neglected and even betrayed, they all dissolved when she was in the arms of her man.

For to Josie, love and sex were one. And she couldn't live without either. A soft, warm, affectionate woman, she enjoyed the act of love immensely. Often in the midst of love-making she would cry with sheer ecstacy. And as she got older, there seemed to be no diminishing of the urge or the ecstacy.

A small, slim woman with a good figure still, she smiled a lot and laughed a lot and admitted to herself that she was truly happy. Why not, indeed, for she had a good man, good children, and darling grandchildren. And she was needed, she knew, by them all.

She had been lucky, oh, so lucky, she often told herself. She'd enjoyed love and good health for years. The fact that they'd not been able to afford many of the things that her better-off friends could afford had never bothered her. She'd been used to doing without. The first Doblins came to Canada from Ulster in 1847 to escape the potato famine, and, like many other native Ulstermen, had experienced hard times as they established themselves in the new land. They'd had bad times, the last being during the Great Depression when her father had lost his job at the insurance company where he'd worked for years.

Besides, Josie had her priorities straight. A good man and a good family were worth far more than anything money could buy.

She'd kissed her son-in-law good-bye at the airport and, instead of loading him down with a lot of advice and admonitions, simply said, "Good luck, Herb. I'm sure Helen will manage just fine."

"I don't know how to thank you for being here," Herb had said. "It, well, it meant everything."

"There was no place else I could be," Josie had said, and kissed him again.

When he'd gone, she sat in the waiting room until her flight was called and thought of home. How good it would be to be held in Ranse's strong arms again. It made her squirm a little in her seat.

The flight was called and she got onto the plane and took her seat next to the window in the non-smoking section. As the people came down the aisle towards her, she tried to decide which of them she'd like as a seatmate. There was a wispy woman with a cranky baby. Oh, Lord, let her pass. She did. A pompous-looking man with a briefcase. She couldn't take him, either. He passed. A friendly-looking coloured woman; Josie hoped she would stop, but she didn't.

A man of about her own age, who looked something like David Niven. He would do nicely, Josie thought, but the man passed. Three others came, but nobody stopped. And then, from behind, she heard a voice.

"By Jove, this must be it after all. I went right past."

It was the man who looked like David Niven. He smiled at her and said, "How do you do? It appears we are to be seatmates."

114

He folded his topcoat and shoved it into the compartment above the seats. "And I just had that thing cleaned and pressed," he said.

"Well, you can always count on an airplane trip to take care of those little problems."

"Indeed one can. Do you know, I noticed you in the waiting room and I hoped I might get to sit beside you."

Josie laughed her musical laugh. "A masher. And at my age."

He looked at her with amusement and appreciation. "Yep. You most certainly have me up. Actually, though, I've never used that line before."

Nor this one, Josie thought, but she felt good. It wasn't every woman who, at fifty-eight, could bring forth a line.

"Please don't let me stop you," she said.

Shortly after the plane took off, the stewardess came along the aisle pushing a cart full of drinks, leaned over them and inquired, "Anything from the bar?"

"Yes," the stranger said. "I'd like a double scotch and soda, no ice, and this young lady will have . . . ." He smiled expectantly.

Oh, what the heck, Josie thought. He seems awfully nice and what can happen to a grandmother on an aircraft? "I'd like a scotch and soda, too, a single, with lots of ice," she said.

The gentleman's eyebrows shot up and he said, "Aha, very good."

When the drinks had been poured and paid for, the gentleman said, "My name is Allenby. James Allenby."

"I'm pleased to meet you, Mr. Allenby. Mine is Josie McGruber, Mrs. Josie McGruber, and if you have nothing better to do, I'd like to show you some pictures of my new grandchildren."

"Delighted."

"I'm most grateful," Josie told him, "that you didn't say I looked too young to be a grandmother, or anything foolish like that."

"I didn't say it because it wouldn't be true. And I resolved when I sat down here to tell the truth. Here's to truth." He raised his glass and took a good, big mouthful.

Josie raised hers and took a tiny sip. "To truth." She set her drink on the tray and dug into her purse to produce a folder of snapshots. "Here they are."

"Hmmm, fine-looking babies. Twins! Boys?"

"One of each. Now they have their family. If they're smart."

"Yes indeed." He took his wallet out and produced a picture of a fine-looking woman of about Josie's age.

"Oh, how nice," Josie said, with real enthusiasm. "Is this your wife?"

"She was my wife," James Allenby said quietly. "She died just over six months ago."

"Oh, I'm so sorry." She laid her hand gently on his arm.

"Yes. So am I. But I'm beginning to get over it a little." He took another pull of his drink. "And that's all there is to tell about me. How about you?"

Airplanes and trains, Josie thought. What is it about them that promotes this instant rapport? She had told people–complete strangers–things on planes and trains that she'd never told anyone else. It was the anonymity of it. You knew you would never see them again, and that probably they'd forget what you told them in their eagerness to tell you something. A plane seat was something like a confessional.

"You live in Toronto?" he asked.

"Oh, no. We did, for thirty years, but when Ranse retired we moved to Muskoka. And we love it. So different from the city, where Ranse was always on call, day or night . . . ."

"Don't tell me, a preacher."

Josie laughed quietly. "Gracious, do I look like a preacher's wife? I'm sorry. You're not a preacher, are you?"

"No indeed."

"Ranse was a detective. In fact he was chief of detectives in Toronto until he retired."

This appeared to interest Allenby very much. "And now he lives in Muskoka. Where in Muskoka?"

"On Wigwam Lake, near the town of Port Perkins. I

don't suppose you've ever heard of either one of them."

James Allenby sat for a moment thinking. "Port Perkins. Didn't I read somewhere about a bank robbery there?"

"Yes, that's right. It happened while I was away, but it was on the radio. Imagine. Somebody just walked into the bank and stuck it up. I don't know if they ever caught the person who did it. Probably."

"Probably. So, your husband is retired."

"Yes. And he hates it. A man as active as he was, and doing exciting work."

"What does he do now?"

"Fishes a little, putters around the place building this and fixing that. And he grumbles a lot."

"Don't we all?"

"It's so hard on a man who retires. I don't suppose he'll ever get used to it. And then there's the pension. When they were first negotiating it, it seemed large enough for us to live on comfortably. But now. Well, with inflation it's–Ranse says–about one quarter of what it would have been."

Allenby stopped the stewardess and asked for another drink. "Would you like one? Hey, you've scarcely touched it."

"But I'm enjoying it. Could I have more ice?"

"Of course. Does your husband take part in any community affairs?"

"Oh, yes. He umpires ball games–he used to play a lot–and he goes to the Legion."

"A veteran, eh?"

"Yes, we met when he was in the navy. Provost Corps." Josie fished into her purse again and produced some worn snapshots in a celluloid holder. "There he is in his uniform. And there's our wedding picture."

"Very nice. As they say, a handsome couple. And who's this with the beard in this picture?"

"That's Ranse, too. Taken just a few months ago."

"Still a fine-looking man. And what a smashing beard."

"Do you like it? I don't know if I do or not. When he

first grew it I scarcely recognized him. Amazing how a beard can change a man's appearance."

"Yes, indeed."

"Ranse said he always wanted one. When he was in the theatre, he liked playing parts of men with beards. Like Sheridan Whiteside."

"Oh yes, in *The Man Who Came to Dinner*. When was he in the theatre?"

"Just about all the time. Little Theatre, you see. He was very good. As a matter of fact–no, I guess I shouldn't tell you this."

"I promise not to tell a soul."

"Of course. You'll forget everything I've told you once we part. That's the way it is with airplane friendships."

"You're right. So why not tell me?" He said it in such an offhand, friendly way that Josie felt foolish about not telling him.

"It's nothing. Just that he always thought that when he retired he'd write detective plays. He tried, for a CBC series, but, well, it didn't work."

"He gave it up?"

"Oh, he tried hard. But finally it was too discouraging. And so he quit."

"Pity."

"I have a son-in-law who is a detective, too." Josie went on, and from there she went to her other daughter and her other grandchildren. James Allenby was a good listener. He was greatly interested in everything Josie said, laughed heartily at her stories about the children and her early days of marriage. Josie could feel him relaxing beside her. Before she realized it, the captain announced that they were over Thunder Bay. "But you haven't told me anything about yourself," she said, half reproachfully.

"Nothing much to tell."

"Are you retired?"

"No such luck."

"Well?"

"Well."

"I know you're not a preacher, but what do you do?"

"Nothing very interesting. I work for an insurance company."

"You do? My father worked for an insurance company–up until the thirties, that is, and then he lost his job. That was such a terrible time. I was just a little girl then, and it didn't affect me so much. But I remember the look on Mother's face when Daddy told her."

"Did you know your husband then? Before the war, I mean."

"Gracious no. Were you in the services?"

"Oh yes, indeed. Pretty hard to avoid it when bombs were dropping on your country."

"Of course. The navy?"

"No, not the navy."

He didn't volunteer any more information, and Josie suddenly realized that he hadn't really told her very much. Something mysterious about him. And she'd told him practically her life's history, and then some. Ranse always said she was too trustful of strangers, that some day she'd run into a slick con-man and get taken.

The plane was beginning its descent, and the captain's voice told them that they'd be landing in ten minutes.

The stewardess came by, picking up glasses and checking seat belts and putting up trays. She took Josie's glass, still half full of watery whiskey.

"Well, it's been most pleasant, Mr. Allenby, and thank you for the drink."

"Much more than just pleasant. Quite the most super trip I've ever had on an airplane."

"Oh, that's nice," Josie said, and then she added something that only a person like her could say without offence, because it was so obviously said out of compassion and real concern. "I hope you will find a real nice person to live with, soon."

Somewhat startled, Allenby answered quickly and with utmost frankness: "Well, I'd never even thought of it before, but now . . . ."

The plane was touching down, and Josie had no time to

wonder what he'd been going to say. When the plane had rolled to a stop, Allenby stood up, retrieved his coat, held out his hand, and said, with great warmth, "Thank you for your company. It has been most pleasant."

"Yes, indeed, and good luck."

He was gone down the crowded aisle. Josie sighed. Such a nice man, and she'd never see him again. That's the way it was with travelling friendships.

CHAPTER THIRTEEN

When Ranse McGruber awoke at six o'clock on the morning of September fifth, he realized that he had been dreaming of Madelaine, dreaming of her as he'd seen her in the water, in her bikini; as she was in his room removing the wet bikini, and coming into his arms, her bare body cool and damp, the black pubic hair damp and curling; the feel of her, the smell of her, the touch of her. For a moment he lay on his back, relishing the dream. Would he ever, he wondered, stop dreaming of her?

He got out of bed, spoke harshly to his rigid member, and struggled into his shorts. It was a warm morning and so he left it at that. After visiting the bathroom, he went into the kitchen, turned on the stove and heated water for coffee.

Today he would meet Josie at the airport. It was six weeks since she'd left, and the place looked like it. That bachelor look, as she described it, with everything left out handy. Vitamin pills on the table, where he would remember them. When he put them away, he often forgot to get them out again. Magazines and papers on the floor where they fell after he'd read them. No dirty dishes in the sink, but the sink had that uncared-for look that it never had under Josie's management.

After his breakfast, he set about tidying the place, man fashion. He even found a dust cloth and waved it at the television set and the buffet and the arms of the chairs, disturbing the dust but removing little of it. The house retained its untidy look.

As with his life. It, too, had become untidy and dusty since Josie had left. When she went, he was a bored, restless sixty-one-year-old with a half-formed plan in his head. A devoted, constant husband who hadn't strayed from the strict marital path in years. A plant going to seed, gradually and relentlessly. A man of honour, of trust, who, more often than not, told the truth. Now, he was a confirmed liar, not only telling lies, but living a lie. A wayward husband who dreamed of the buxom beauty of a thirty-year-old woman. A fraud and a criminal.

Well, what the hell, he thought, the world is full of frauds: politicians who lie and play dirty tricks and stonewall; bankers who urge people to borrow money they can't afford to borrow; doctors who perform unneeded operations for the sake of the fees; a government that takes out television ads telling people they can win a million dollars, when their chances of doing so are so infinitessimal as to be non-existent; evangelists who filch money from the poor with promises of eternal life; businessmen who lie in their teeth and steal from their own companies. A world full of liars. Well, he thought, if you can't lick 'em, join 'em.

He had crossed over, he told himself. Joined the majority. Left the ranks of the good and the meek. Blessed are the meek for they shall inherit the dirt. He was a man of substance. Sitting there on Rattlesnake Island, just waiting to be picked up, was a veritable fortune. It was easy, he thought, to cross over. One small step for greed.

But the complications! Ah, there was the rub. He had complicated his life as well as changed it. There was Madelaine to think of. The girl of the golden skin. The girl who may have an inkling of his secret. The smart thing to do was put her out of his mind. Women like her were trouble. He knew that. He'd seen it many times. Brilliant crooks whose hormones took over from their brains, and who did stupid things.

Like Ranse McGruber, in pursuit of Madelaine.

122

He prepared the house for his absence with care. Closed all the windows, turned off the water pump and the hot-water heater, locked the doors, knowing, as he did so, that any experienced thief could easily gain entrance. But who would bother? There wasn't much here worth stealing.

After he backed out the driveway and ascertained that no car was coming, Ranse pulled to the side of the road, got out of the car, walked back to the driveway, and, with a branch, brushed loose sand over the marks of his tires. If there were fresh marks there when he got back, he'd know he'd had a visitor. A policeman is always wary.

He drove the Nova along the winding sideroad to the highway and followed it to Highway 11, the main road to Toronto. He drove a careful 80 km/h, which was the speed limit. Ranse rarely drove faster than the legal limit. He hated breaking the law.

The highway took him south, past filling stations, garishly decorated "trading posts" and motels. He tried to keep his mind on Josie and their thousands of good times together, but his mind kept turning to Madelaine and their one time together. Well, he thought, as he turned off Highway 401 onto the airport road, it was Josie he was meeting and he'd better be on his guard about what he said, and did. Being on guard would be his lot from here on in.

He was still cautioning himself when he pulled into the airport parking garage and walked across the overhead bridge to Terminal 2, where the Air Canada passengers assembled. The first person he saw when he got off the escalator at the Arrivals Level was his daughter Susie, looking very smart in a green pant suit. And behind her, his son-in-law Zeke.

"Dad!" She rushed up to him and gave him a big hug and kiss. "You look wonderful!"

That was Susie. Always saying the right thing.

"Feel great," he said, returning her hug. "Fishing trip did me good."

He disengaged himself from Susie and shook Zeke's

hand, noting, as always, his son-in-law's firm grip. Firm was the word for Zeke. A firm mind in a firm body. A good example of the modern detective–well educated, well adjusted, and unemotional. And devoted to his profession. There would never be any corruption connected with Zeke. And steadfast. He'd arrest his own mother, Ranse thought ruefully, if he thought she were guilty. Or his father-in-law.

"Look," Ranse suggested, "it's almost three-quarters of an hour to plane time. How about we have a couple in the lounge?"

The others agreed, and they found their way through the crowd to the lounge and managed to get a small table in the corner.

"Well, how was your stay at the cottage?" Ranse asked when they'd got their drinks.

"Just fine, Ranse," Zeke said. "And by the way, thanks."

"Do any fishing?"

Susie snorted. "Spent all his time in town, talking to people about the bank robbery."

"Oh?"

"Not all my time. But it is a fascinating case."

Case? Now he was calling it a case. His case?

"How so?" Ranse asked.

"Well, it just doesn't make sense. A man robs a bank, walks out into the street and disappears." Zeke rubbed his chin. "In broad daylight. Street full of people."

"Maybe that's why he could disappear," Ranse suggested.

"Yeah, safety in numbers. And that chain on the door. He must have known about that."

"Don't robbers case the joint before they pull a job?" Susie suggested facetiously.

Zeke missed the sarcasm. "Yeah, but I've a feeling this must have been a local person."

"But nobody in the bank recognized him," Ranse suggested guardedly. "And they get to know all the local people."

"Dad, please, don't encourage him," Susie pleaded. "It's got nothing to do with us, or with Zeke. I can't understand why he keeps harping on it!"

"It's a crime. And crime is my job. You know, Ranse, the thing that strikes me about this?"

"What?"

"It's too perfect. Too well planned. Too, well, intelligent."

Damn! Why doesn't he leave it alone? Ranse thought.

"No local hoodlum pulled this off," Zeke went on. "Had to be somebody who'd thought a lot about it. Take that crazy costume he had on."

"Costume?"

"Yeah. According to the manager, who saw him best, he had on a suit of coveralls, rubber boots and a crazy hat. You know, he could have had a completely different outfit on underneath that!" Zeke sipped his gin and tonic thoughtfully. "But what I don't understand is how he could disguise his face."

And that, my friend, is something you will never figure out in your logical brain, Ranse thought. You know all about a person disguising himself by putting on a beard, but you never heard of anyone doing it by taking off a beard.

"May I have another?" Susie asked. "This sort of talk always makes me thirsty."

"I guess we have time. How about you, Zeke?"

"No, thanks. One's my limit. Got some calls to make this afternoon."

"Interesting case?" Ranse asked.

"Pretty cut and dried. Warehouse manager stealing from his own establishment, and planting phony clues all over the place."

"Will you get him?"

"Yeah, but it won't do much good."

"Why do you say that?" Susie asked.

"What do you think? Here's a respected man, good citizen, big house in Thorncrest, church member, clean record. He'll get a slap on the wrist."

"Whereas," Susie said with feeling, "if he were black and poor and had stolen a hubcap as a kid, he'd go to jail for five years."

"Exactly," Ranse said. "Seems to be how the system works. If you can afford a good lawyer, you can get away with about anything. But a prostitute on the street . . . ."

"Dad, I never heard you talk this way before."

"It's the truth, though," Zeke said.

"Then how can you go on arresting people who . . . ?"

"Because it's my job. The law may be an ass, as somebody said, but that's not my department. I'm paid to catch law-breakers. And I'm pretty good at it."

"Dad," Susie cut in, before Ranse could reply to this self-estimate.

"Yeah?"

"How does it feel to have two more grandchildren? All at once?"

He'd never thought much about it. So preoccupied with other things that he'd never even inquired about the new twins' weights. "Uh, am I suppose to feel something?"

"Well, yes. Two sets of twins in one family. That's something."

He thought about it, and all he could think of was responsibility. New lives on this earth, new responsibility for somebody. No wonder, he thought, that young people are opting out of having children.

"Yes, yes, of course." The time had come to start lying. "I'm delighted. Have they got names for them yet?"

"Dad! Of course. Josie and Ranse."

"You mean there's one of each?"

"Somebody must have told you that!"

"I suppose somebody may have."

"Well, it's a good thing we are having this talk before Mother arrives. Josie weighed in at five pounds, ten and a half ounces, and Ranse at an even six."

"I see. What else do you know about them?"

"Both strong and healthy."

Zeke was looking at his watch. "Time to go. That plane will be landing any minute."

She came rushing through the glass doors towards him, a small, trim figure in a pant suit that fitted her figure magnificently. She was smiling her broad, happy smile that completely took over her face, obliterating the laugh lines at the corners of her mouth and eyes. She flung herself into his arms and said, "Oh darling, I've missed you so much. It's so good to be home!"

He kissed her warm, soft lips, but he felt nothing. As she squirmed in his arms and smiled up at his face and asked, "Have you missed me?" he could only answer, "Sure have."

But she didn't notice. She turned to her daughter and son-in-law and embraced them with her love.

CHAPTER FOURTEEN

"How was your flight?" Ranse asked, as they pulled out of the parking lot of the Food Basket, an immense supermarket on Highway 11 that catered to summer people driving north. They'd stocked up on vegetables and fruits and staples, and on natural peanut butter that the customer made himself by dumping peanuts into a grinder and catching the butter in a plastic container as it emerged from the other end. The peanut butter was Ranse's passion, and he never missed a chance to get a few cartons.

"Oh, it was fine," Josie said. "I sat with the most interesting man."

"Uh huh."

Josie always managed to find an interesting man, Ranse thought. She attracted them, like honey attracts flies. Not just a cliché, Josie was like honey. Soft and sweet and completely desirable. And she had this genuine interest in other people. Never failed to strike up a conversation. And people confided in her, responded to her warmth, told her about themselves.

"It's a funny thing about the people you meet on airplanes," Josie mused. "An instant rapport."

"Yeah. This interesting man. Did he buy you a drink?"

"Yes, but I offered to buy him one in return. Well, you know, it's not right to accept things from strangers."

"But he didn't seem like a stranger."

"No, he didn't. And he needed so much to talk to somebody."

"A sympathetic ear."

"Yes. You see he'd lost his wife. She died just six months ago."

Lost his wife. Ranse sometimes permitted himself to think of that, of losing a partner, a mate, somebody with whom you were comfortable, who was as much a part of you as you were yourself.

"I suppose he fell for you," Ranse said, only half jokingly.

"Oh, Ranse, what a thing to say!" He knew without looking at her that she'd be blushing with pleasure. "An old lady like me."

Ranse didn't answer. His mind darted off again along the now-familiar path. As Josie chatted on happily about Helen and Herb, their home and friends, and the new babies, he scarcely heard what she was saying. Normally, he would have been interested because Helen had always been his favourite; but now she seemed somehow remote and detached from him, as though she were part of a past that was gone. If Josie noticed that he asked no questions, made no comment, she didn't mention it.

When they turned off the highway onto Muskoka 75 and the road wound between the maples, oaks, birches and sumacs, just beginning to get a tinge of red, Josie sighed happily.

"This is so nice. Oh, the prairie is nice too, especially this time of year," she added, unable ever to indulge in the adversary attitude so common to Canadians. "But I did miss the trees."

"Yeah, it's hard to beat Muskoka in the fall," Ranse agreed.

When they reached the driveway, Ranse stopped before turning in and inspected the loose sand he'd spread. No tracks.

"Why did you do that?" Josie asked when he got back into the car.

"Just making sure we didn't have any visitors."

"Oh, your suspicious policeman's mind! This isn't the city, you know."

"Been some break-ins in the area this summer."

"Really? Here?"

"Yeah, here. Crime doesn't play favourites. It's everywhere."

"Yes, like that terrible robbery at the bank. Imagine! In broad daylight, too."

"Small banks are the easiest to knock over," he said without thinking.

"Well, I hope they catch whoever did it and put him in jail for a good long time."

"Amen."

Ranse followed his wife down the path and over the patio to the front door of the cottage. He marvelled again at the way her little round backside moved with her strides.

And he felt something else. Something more subtle. That Josie had missed her man in a more vital way than just having someone to talk to. And always, over all the years, Ranse had missed her even more than she missed him. But now he felt absolutely nothing.

He thought of the many times when, returning from a trip, he could hardly wait to get hold of her. As in the old joke about the returning soldier: "The second thing I did was take off my pack." It had always been such a great time for both of them. The excited rush together. Nothing like it in this world.

He opened the door for her, and she brushed past him. He followed with the suitcases. When he set them down, she turned to him, threw her arms around him, and planted a very big, moist kiss on his lips.

"Did you miss me?"

"Sure did."

"How much?"

"Well, you know, a lot."

She kissed him again, rubbing her body against his, then drew back. "What's the matter, darling?"

"Nothing. Nothing at all."

That was just it. Nothing. For the first time since he had met her, there was no response. And she knew it. Everything about her suddenly changed. Josie was not a woman to question a thing like this. Her female pride, which was great, would never permit it. She pulled away and was all business.

"Well, the place looks, uh, very good."

"Yeah, I kept the dishes washed up." He felt awful. "Made the bed, too."

"Wonderful. Well, the first thing for me is a shower, and then get into some more comfortable clothes and get to work."

"Work?"

"Yes, my flower bed. I noticed it as we came in. It does indeed need work."

"Yeah, well."

"Oh, I didn't expect you to do anything with it." She went into the bedroom.

He didn't follow. And he knew that he didn't want to be around when she stepped out of the shower. "Yeah, I've got some things to do down at the dock. Boathouse needs looking into."

The lake was beautiful, tranquil and beautiful. Not a motorboat, not even a sailboat. Nothing. Most of the cottages hidden by trees. Peace. But not contentment. Was this another change in his life since you-know-what? Was he never again to feel any kind of tranquillity or contentment? Well, the dead are tranquil, the dead are content. To live means to be restless, unhappy, wanting, troubled, filled with stress. That's what he'd been missing. The stress.

He went to the door of the boathouse with his key in his hand, but he didn't need it. When he fitted it into the lock, it turned with no resulting click. The door had been left unopened?

Impossible. He never went away and left the boathouse unlocked. Or was this another sign of age, forgetting to lock things? He quickly pushed the door open, and then, policeman-wise, stood and carefully looked around.

Everything was in its place. Maybe too much in its place. That bait bucket. Had it been moved? Sweat gathered in his armpits and trickled down his side. Somebody had been here. Somebody very careful, but not careful enough to lock the door. Who?

Cautiously he inspected the rest of the boathouse and the boat. There were other small signs. The cushion of the rear seat had been lifted and the space beneath it inspected. Nothing was taken. His tool box was still there, even the crescent wrench he'd left beside it. Nothing stolen, but somebody had been searching the boat. Why?

He went to the dock. Canoe still there, hadn't been touched. Of course, no one would hide anything under an inverted canoe. He walked back from the dock into the edge of the woods. Yes, somebody else had walked back there, too. Looking for what? Signs of something buried?

He went back to the cottage. Josie turned from the kitchen sink which she'd been scouring, hard, and asked, "Ranse, were you looking for something in the back of my closet?"

So somebody had been in the house, too. "Oh? I don't remember."

"Somebody was looking in there. That box of Christmas stuff has been opened."

"Eh?" Think fast, Ranse. You don't want her to know about this. "Oh yeah, I was looking in that. Thought maybe one of the balls might make a float."

"Ranse?"

"Well, you know . . . ."

She put down her cloth. "Ranse, I just don't believe that. An old fisherman like you."

He laughed uneasily. Lies, lies, lies. How do you keep from tripping yourself up? "You're right, it was the extension cord I was after."

"But there's none in there."

Relief. If there had been, he'd have had to account for it, or for why he hadn't taken it. "I know that now."

She went back to her scouring, even harder, with a frown creasing her forehead. Something was wrong and she knew it.

Ranse went into the bedroom and checked carefully. Somebody had been here, all right. Bureau drawers were just a little too tidy. A pair of socks he'd had out, and put back again without wearing, was now under another pair of socks, instead of on top, where it should have been. He opened his wife's vanity drawer and inspected the jewellery box. Not much there, but any self-respecting burglar would have taken the two gold rings, heirlooms from Josie's mother; not worth much before, but now, with gold at $340 an ounce, certainly worth taking.

The evidence of a search was more obvious in his study. Somebody had carefully removed all the books from the shelves and replaced them. Somebody who wasn't in a hurry. Somebody who knew he–or she–had a full, uninterrupted day. Somebody who knew he'd be going to the city that day. He searched his mind. Only one person knew that. No, two–Madelaine and Willie.

Willie, of course. He came by boat or perhaps even swam around the point. And this put an entirely new light on Mr. Willie. He was no ordinary crook, but an experienced, even trained searcher. So, who was he, and where had he learned his trade? And more important, what was he doing here? Ranse felt a momentary twinge of panic.

And then it left him. Of course Willie had found nothing. Not the vaguest clue. Or had he? Ranse hurried down to the garage. He found indications of a search there, but the spot where the box key was hidden appeared untouched. He took his knife and dug into the plastic wood, removed the key and attached it to his own keyring. That's where keys should be. He didn't remember what half the other keys were for. Carefully, he repaired the crack with more plastic wood and left the garage. There were no clues anywhere. He knew that. Whoever had spent the day searching the place had wasted his time.

Ranse sat and watched a rerun of "Get Smart," and for a while forgot everything else.

Josie seemed to be in a work fit. She scrubbed the kitchen floor, made a big dinner and, by the time the rerun of "Hollywood Squares" came on, he had a hard time to get her to sit down and have a drink. After a rum and Coke she relaxed somewhat, and fished out the pictures of the new grandchildren. To Ranse they looked like babies; but Josie saw much more in them than that. Their features were recognizable as those belonging to different members of her family. "Uncle John had a chin just like that." Ranse couldn't detect any sign of a chin. He wondered idly what Herb's family had to say about the twins.

After dinner there was the regular Wednesday night baseball game. The Blue Jays and Baltimore. As usual, both he and Josie ruled up their pages and kept a box score.

But it wasn't much of a game and Ranse found himself back in Christie Pits in 1938, playing for the Toronto policemen's baseball team. How he loved those games! He would crouch behind home plate where he could see everything that was going on on the field, calling the pitches, cutting off runners at second. One evening he hit a grand slam homer in the last of the ninth when the team was three runs down. That was his greatest moment in baseball, perhaps the greatest moment in his entire life! A rookie on the team, and a grand slam homer. Then, after the game, at the Brunswick House on Bloor Street, drinking beer with the other players and their girls.

It was Nancy Shields then. Ah, Nancy. He'd borrow his dad's Buick and drive out to High Park. And they'd make love on the soft grass under the huge oaks. Ah, Nancy. The thing then was not to get a dose or make the girl pregnant. That was their watchword. The French letters took care of that. Besides, no one ever got a dose from Nancy.

And then there were Patty and Gwen and Dolores and Yvonne. They were all great girls. All good sports. But they all lacked something. A guy could have a lot of fun in Toronto in those days. Then he'd seen Josie and it all changed. He wanted her and nothing else, at least that is what he'd thought. She was the kind of girl he'd always wanted, the kind of girl everybody wanted. And so they were married, and the children came along, easily and naturally. There was never any idea of not having kids. Not with Josie. She loved babies, all babies, and especially her own.

He glanced over at her now and saw that she was tired.

"I think I'll go to bed now," she said. "It's been a long day. Jet lag or something."

She got up, tidied the table in front of the couch, came over and kissed him lightly on the forehead. There would be, he knew, no more sexual overtures from Josie. They would have to come from him, and he knew they weren't going to come.

As the game dragged on, he could hear her getting ready for bed in the bathroom and then going into their room. After the game he watched the evening news, and then a late movie. He went to sleep in his chair, and when he got up and went to bed, Josie was sound asleep. He didn't waken her.

CHAPTER FIFTEEN

On the morning of Friday, September 7, Ranse McGruber awoke from a bad dream. It was a dream he'd had before; in it he was surrounded by a menacing group of people. He could never see exactly who they were, or what they wanted with him, but he felt terror in their presence. Even their faces were obscure, and they came and went like mist, now pressing in on him, now receding. As he came awake, he noted that it was getting light outside and Josie was still sound asleep. The luminous dial on his watch read 6:47.

Carefully he extricated himself from the covers, gathered his clothing, and slipped out into the dining area. It was chilly in the cottage and he turned up the electric heat. To hell with the expense. At least when Josie awakened, the house would be warm.

He took his down-lined hunting jacket from its peg on the kitchen wall, put it on, and went quietly out the front door. The water of the lake was calm as a bath and over it lay a heavy mist. He went down to the dock and looked out towards Rattlesnake Island, which was obscured by the mist. A fortune lay out there, or did it? How could he know that someone had not accidentally uncovered his treasure trove and was, even now, living it up in Key West or some other tropical paradise? He had a strong urge to get into his canoe and paddle out to see, but he knew it would be an unwise thing to do. There might be fishermen out there, or kids looking for blackberries.

Besides, how could he explain it to Josie? Everything had changed since she came home.

But he wasn't thinking about Josie. He was thinking of Madelaine and Antigua. He'd never forgotten Runaway Beach, where he and Josie had spent an Easter week shortly after both the girls had left home. The long stretch of sand and the little cottages. He and Josie had a lot of fun in their cottage. Rum at two-fifty a bottle, and how Josie loved rum. Walking on the beach, dancing to the marimba band, drinking at Buccaneer Cove, but mostly making love in the cottage, with the blackbirds outside screeching "*Meet Macraeee.*" He tried to think of him and Josie again in the cottage, but it kept coming out as him and Madelaine.

He walked back to the house and found Josie up and making breakfast. She was full of stories of Helen and the babies and Helen's friends. But Ranse could tell that underneath the smiles and enthusiasm there was bewilderment and hurt. And there was still nothing he could do about it.

At about ten o'clock Josie called him down off the ladder, where he was repairing the electric wire along the edge of the roof to prevent icing.

"It's the telephone, dear, Mr. Allenby."

"Who?"

"Allenby! It's the man I met on the plane! You know."

"Oh, yeah. The one that looks like Peter Ustinov."

"David Niven."

"Of course. But why is he phoning me? Going to ask for your hand?"

"Ranse!"

He was in the house now and picking up the phone.

"Hello."

"Mr. McGruber?" The voice was crisp, with an English accent.

"Yeah."

"My name is Allenby. James Allenby. I'm in Port Perkins."

"You are?"

137

"Yes. And I should very much like to talk with you, if you have time, that is."

"What about?"

"I'd rather not say over the phone. Your wife, uh, told me something about you, and I have a proposition that might interest you."

"Oh?"

"Could you possibly pop in here? I'm at the bank."

Bank. Why in hell would he be at the bank? "Uh, yeah. Look, why don't you pop out here? My wife is dying to see you."

"Well, all right." The voice had gone a bit cold. "I should very much like to see her, too. Charming woman."

"Yeah. Well, here's how you get here." He gave the directions and hung up.

"Ranse," Josie said, "why did you say I was dying to see him?"

"What's more to the point, what did you tell him about me?" His tone was sharper than he intended. But he'd been jolted.

"Well, you know, dear, airplane conversation. I was just talking."

"You talk too damned much!"

"Ranse! What a thing to say!"

"Well, you do. Especially if there's a man involved."

Her face had gone white and her lips were firm. "What in the world do you mean?"

"Just that. You're always striking up conversations with men. Attractive men."

Josie didn't answer, but left the room with her head high. The bedroom door slammed shut. This was as close as Josie could come to a fight with her spouse. She didn't know how to fight. She knew how to be friendly and warm and loving and funny and even flirtatious, but she had absolutely no talent for being mean or nasty. And because of this, she was terribly vulnerable.

Ranse had known of this vulnerability since he first met her, and had always been careful not to take advantage of it. He could count the fights they'd had over their thirty-six years of marriage, and they had all been short. Ranse could never stay mad long, and the making up had always been particularly sweet.

But now he was still angry. Angry and alarmed. The bank? What the hell was this cove Allenby doing at the bank? And why did he want to see Ranse? Could he be investigating the robbery? But why phone Ranse?

He went outside and sat on a patio chair. The thing to do is wait and see. Jump to no conclusions, and above all, don't panic! He thought of a case in which he'd been involved. When he'd gone to talk to a potential witness, the man had panicked and given himself away, thereby solving the case himself. Ranse wouldn't do that.

When the rented car pulled into the driveway and somebody got out, Ranse shouted, "Over here on the patio."

The man who came around the corner of the house didn't look like David Niven or anybody else. He was tall and lean, all right, but his face was completely neutral. It revealed nothing. Ranse had seen a face like that once before, in the wardroom of H.M.C.S. *York* during the war, when a civilian who was whispered to be with British Intelligence stopped in on his way somewhere.

Ranse stood up and extended his hand. "How do you do? I'm Ranse McGruber. You'll excuse my torn shirt, but I was doing some work on the roof when you called."

"Not at all, old man. Good of you to see me." He took Ranse's hand. His grip was neither firm nor weak. Neutral, like his smile.

Ranse motioned him to a patio chair. "Can I get you a drink?"

"Most kind. Bit early in the day for me. I'll pass for the present. Nice place you have here."

"Yes, we like it."

"The lake is beautiful. My first experience with Muskoka lakes. Pretty as any I've seen."

"I suppose you've seen lots in England."

"Oh yes, and Switzerland, and Italy, and of course Germany."

"Of course?"

"Stationed there for a spell after the war. At that time I was still in the Foreign Service. But that's all past now, thank God. Now I do investigation work for an insurance company."

"I see." Don't be too curious, Ranse warned himself. I'm dealing with a real pro here. Big league.

Josie came out onto the patio then and Allenby leaped to his feet with a real smile on his face. "By jove, this is a pleasure."

Ranse noticed that Josie had put on her most attractive pant suit. And just a touch of makeup. She looked great.

"Yes, of course. You two have met."

Josie smiled warmly. "But I never thought we'd meet again."

"Strange things happen. I'm never surprised at what turns events can take."

"I've put the coffee on. It'll be ready in a moment, so, if you'll excuse me." Josie went back inside.

"Charming woman, your wife."

"I've noticed."

"Yes, of course." He sat down again. "Mr. McGruber, I'll lay my cards on the table. I'm investigating the robbery that took place in the bank last month, for my insurance company who bore the loss."

"Uh, yeah. I know about the robbery, of course, but isn't that, well, small potatoes for you? I mean, a small branch . . . ."

"In a way, I suppose. But there have been a number of similar robberies in other small branches within the past year. They all follow a pattern."

Ranse was alert. Something told him this wasn't exactly so. "A pattern?"

"Yes, not the ordinary thing where some inebriated johnny pulls a stocking over his face and sticks up the bank. The local police solve those in no time. So many clues left about that my Aunt Fanny could catch them."

Ranse laughed. "I know the kind."

"Yes, I'm sure you do. Your wife told me all about you

and something of your record as a detective. Laying that Edmonton chappie by the heels was good."

"You mean the famous Air Canada Burglar who hopped a plane in Edmonton, robbed a bank in Toronto, and was back in Edmonton on the next plane. Just a neat little business trip by a typical businessman."

"Yes, that one. How did you get on to him?"

"A hunch, and then a lot of hard work checking airline schedules."

"Ah, yes, hunches. Where would we be without them? You don't happen to have a hunch about this robbery in town?"

Now it comes, Ranse thought. A perfectly innocent question. He will have found out everything there is to find out about the robbery. "No, not really. Why?"

"Well, I thought perhaps, being a detective—"

"Retired detective."

"Quite, but one never loses the urge to find out, I suppose. Were you in town that afternoon?"

You know damned well I was, Ranse thought. Aloud he said, "Yes, I was. Matter of fact, I was in the bank that day. And I arrived on the scene shortly afterwards."

"Yes, yes. That chappie across the street. With the funny name. Tick, is it?"

"Tipton, Tip Tipton. Runs the drugstore."

"That's the one. He mentioned something about it."

So the investigation has begun. But why is he here? "And you? Do you have any hunches?"

"Well, it's a deuced queer case. I got the complete report, of course. Something about the whole thing bothers me. I'm not just sure what it is, but, before I go any further, I must clear something with you. Why I'm here, actually."

"I've been wondering about that."

At this moment, Josie appeared on the patio with a tray loaded with coffee, mugs, and some little cookies that Ranse must have overlooked while she was away. Josie could always come up with something.

"I'm afraid this isn't much," she smiled. "But I've been away."

"Of course. This looks wonderful." It seemed to Ranse that Allenby's smile was different when he smiled at Josie. More genuine and open.

Josie settled into a wooden chair and sighed contentedly. "My, but I did miss this place! The trees and the lake. I do dearly love lakes. Heavenly."

"I was just remarking to your husband that this is one of the most charming areas I've ever visited."

"We just love it. And we feel so lucky to be able to live here year round."

"It doesn't get, well . . . ."

"Boring?"

"It is a bit remote."

Josie laughed. "Not when you get to know it. There's the church and the Legion, and the quilting club and Mother's Madness."

"I beg your pardon?"

"Mother's Madness? Oh, it's a club for young mothers. They get together every Wednesday and bring their children. Then they do their crafts and hear talks from interesting people. Ranse was one of those. I baby-sit."

Allenby laughed. "I see. Good idea. Must admit I was thinking of something a little more sinister."

While Josie went on explaining how the name Mother's Madness had come about, and describing her other activities in the community, Ranse had a chance to collect his thoughts. He had a notion of what Allenby might be about to propose. He seemed in no hurry to get on with it. He was sitting back in his chair, listening to Josie's ramblings as though they were the most interesting topics in the world. Then he glanced at his watch.

"By jove, it's getting on to eleven. I've almost forgotten my mission."

Josie got up to go. "I'll leave you two alone." She gathered up her tray and went back through the glass doors.

142

Allenby turned to Ranse. "I hate to disturb this tranquillity with thoughts of more worldly matters. But I was about to ask you, Mr. McGruber, if you might assist us with our investigation?"

"Me?"

"Who better? You live here. You know the people. You have experience, and I suspect you don't have as many activities as your wife."

"Well, you're right there. But the police—"

"Yes, of course. The OPP are doing what they can. But I'm convinced that this is more than they can handle. Oh, don't misunderstand. It's just that they haven't the time. You see, I'm convinced this was done by a local person."

"Oh?"

"And a very clever one. It has all those earmarks of a job done by a person whom no one would suspect. Something like your Edmonton case. Probably not a criminal. Not until this job. Previous offenders have all been checked out. I can count on your discretion?"

"Yes, of course."

"There is the possibility that someone in the bank is involved."

"Why do you think that?"

"I don't think it. Or anything else. As I said, it's a very peculiar case. Now, we're prepared to pay you a retainer, just to investigate quietly."

"Quietly?" Ranse snorted. "If I ask one person one question, it will be all over town that I'm on the case. You don't know your small towns."

"Yes, I suppose that's so. Well, we'll come out in the open then. The bank manager will know, and the staff. We could easily arrange for a licence as a private investigator."

"There goes my retirement."

"Is it really that much fun?"

"No. I have been toying with the idea of getting into some sort of security work, perhaps, but what about you?"

"My office is in Toronto. I'll be around."

"I see." Ranse's mind was racing–first, with the relief that there was an explanation for Allenby's visit, then with a sense of the irony of it. Investigate his own crime? And then the old feeling of suspicion and caution. What could this lead to? Maybe he'd be better off to stay right out of it.

"I must admit," Allenby went on, lighting up a pipe, "that the idea for this came to me when I was speaking to your wife on the plane. Then I made a few phone calls yesterday afternoon. Your reputation in Toronto is excellent." He took his pipe from his mouth and half pointed it at Ranse. "And we will pay a rather healthy retainer. Say three thousand a month."

Three thousand a month! Ranse had never made that much when he was working steadily. Of course, salaries had jumped drastically since he left, but he'd never been in on the big money.

"And expenses, of course," Allenby added. "It's not much, I know, in these days of inflation, but I'm afraid it's all we can manage."

"I don't know. Investigating my friends and neighbours."

"But, my dear chap, surely they are as anxious to have this case solved as we are. To paraphrase Barnum: You can't hurt an honest man."

"You can't, eh? I'd like to believe that."

"Well," Allenby stood up. "That's the proposition. Think it over and let me know. Here's my number at the lodge. I'll be there for a few days." He handed Ranse a card. "And I know you won't mention this to anyone."

"Not very likely. Except to my wife. She's quite a talker, as you've seen, but she knows when not to talk, too."

"Good."

Ranse got up and called, "Josie, our guest is leaving."

She came through the doors, went up to Allenby and put both her hands in his. "It was wonderful to see you again, Mr. Allenby. I didn't expect to, you know."

"Well, I hope it's not the last time."

He said his good-byes and left.

"Isn't it strange," Josie said, "my meeting him and then his coming here? I hope I haven't done any harm by telling him . . . ."

"Of course not. I'm sorry I was sharp with you this morning. I really am."

She came over to him and kissed him warmly. "I hate it when we fight. What did Mr. Allenby want? To sell you insurance? I'm bursting to know."

"Tell you later. Want to think about it first. Right now, I'm going to finish fixing that damned roof."

"All right. I have some drawers to clean out. Better start getting ready for winter, I suppose."

She left and went back into the house. Ranse climbed back up his ladder and thought of Madelaine. Did Allenby suspect her?

145

CHAPTER SIXTEEN

"Now, our procedure here will be to go over the robbery, step by step," James Allenby said.

They were standing in the bank manager's office, Allenby, Ranse McGruber, and Parsons. The big clock on the back of the wall said two minutes after ten. It was Saturday and the bank was closed. The investigation had begun.

Ranse McGruber wondered to himself, What am I doing here? After James Allenby had made his proposition and left, Ranse thought about the problem from every possible angle. Then he had told Josie about it.

"He wants you to investigate the robbery?" Her eyes were big. "Why him? Why you?"

"He's in charge of criminal investigations for the insurance company that paid off on the robbery."

"He is? Well, imagine! He never said a thing about that to me."

"Probably didn't get a chance."

"Oh, Ranse. But why you?"

"Well, I'm a detective. He thinks it's a local job."

"But who would do such a thing?" For all her years of being married to a detective, Josie still couldn't imagine why anyone would commit a crime.

"He says it could be anybody, somebody no one would suspect."

"Nobody we know, surely. . . ."

"They'll pay me three thousand a month, plus expenses."

"That's a lot of money! Do you want to do it?"

He didn't want to do it, didn't want to have any part of it, and knew he shouldn't. But three thousand dollars a month! He could sure use that. And if he solved the crime, and got the ten grand reward, it might lead to other jobs with Allenby. Solved the crime! What in hell was he thinking about? If he solved the crime, he'd be in jail!

But the money. If this job had just come along before he robbed the bank. What the hell? If he hadn't robbed the bank, there'd be no job.

But maybe he could solve it, at that. Pin it on somebody. Send an innocent man to jail? No, he'd never do a thing like that. He never had, although he'd been tempted. But all that was changed. In the last few weeks, he'd done a lot of things he'd never done before. The old Ranse McGruber—honest man, crime fighter, straight shooter—was gone. There was a new one here now, a man with different drives, a different ethos, different standards. Nobody could know what dirty tricks this new Ranse McGruber would concoct.

And the money. The irony of it delighted the new Ranse McGruber. Paid to work on his own crime. It also appealed to his sense of the dramatic.

There was another angle, too. If he didn't take the job, they might bring in a hotshot from outside to work on it. This way, he could control the direction the investigation would take, lead them up all sorts of blind alleys. Everything had changed since Allenby came into the case. They knew they were dealing with an unusual criminal, and not just some punk stickup man.

And Allenby, what of him? A devious character, if he'd ever seen one. Super-trained in deviousness. A man to whom nothing was too preposterous to be possible. A man who lived by lies and knew what others were capable of. Did Allenby suspect him already? Was this offer just part of a diabolical plan?

Ranse found the old excitement coming back, the old keenness for the chase, pitting his mind and knowledge against a worthy opponent.

Now, in the bank office, Parsons sighed. "Go over it again? I've been over it ten times already!"

"I know, but you may have missed something. A little thing, no matter how apparently insignificant, that might give us a clue," Allenby said.

"Okay, let's go."

"I'm going to ask you a lot of questions that you may think have nothing to do with the crime. I want to get your mind back to that time, so that you might bring something out of your subconscious that you don't know is there."

"Like hypnotism, you mean?"

"Somewhat the same, but you won't be hypnotized. Now, let's go back to the afternoon of August seventh. You are just back from working after a holiday. What did you do on Monday, the holiday?"

"That's easy. Went fishing."

"Catch any?"

"No. Damned acid rain has ruined the lakes."

"So what time did you get back?"

"Six, seven. No, I know it was just before seven. 'Mary Tyler Moore' was on."

"Good. Now we'll jump to the next day. The day of the robbery. What kind of day was it?"

"Uh." Parsons wrinkled his brow. "Sunny. Yeah, sunny. I remember. I hated to come back to work. Well, you know, not exactly hate."

"Good. Now then, what were you doing just before the robbery?"

"Sitting in the office here, at my desk."

"Uh, huh. Doing what?"

"That's a little tougher. Oh, yeah, going over a loan application."

"Whose?"

"Joe Simpson's, I think. Yeah." He made a face. "Joe's

148

got his well-digging business in a hole. No pun intended.''

Ranse couldn't help guffawing.

"How much money did he want?" Allenby pressed on.

"A lot more than we could give him. Fifty thousand."

"You were going to refuse the loan?" Ranse put in for the first time.

The manager looked startled. "Hey, it couldn't be Joe Simpson!"

"It could be anybody. Don't forget that," Allenby said coldly. "All we know for sure is that somebody came in here and stole two hundred and sixteen thousand dollars."

"But Joe is over six feet tall. And this guy–"

"We'll come to that. Now, did anyone come into the office before the robbery?"

"Let me think. Yes, one of the girls."

"Uh huh. Which one?"

"Which one? That's tough. Let me see. Yeah,. Madelaine."

"Madelaine?"

Ranse noticed some agitation on the manager's face. He and Madelaine?

"She's the dark girl. Rather pretty." He was definitely fidgeting.

"Married?"

"Uh, no. She's the only one of the six girls who isn't married."

"Now think hard. What did she want?"

"What did she want? Some bank business."

"What exactly?"

The manager thought. Ranse watched him. If he'd ever seen anyone seeking for an answer, he was it. "Oh, something about a cheque, I think."

"What about the cheque?"

"Well."

Ranse knew now that he was lying. Why had she come in?

"Go on."

"One of the tourists wanted to cash a cheque for a rather large amount."

"How much exactly?"

"What difference does it make?"

"Maybe none. But somewhere in your head is that figure. Let's see if we can't get it out."

Parsons was thinking. Then his face brightened. "Over two hundred dollars. Yeah, two hundred and four dollars and twenty-six cents. '

"A dividend cheque?"

"Yes, that's right."

"From one of the trust companies?" Ranse could tell that, for the first time, Allenby was leading him on.

"I think so. I forget which one."

"Well, we can check it." It was a throw-away remark, but the effect on the manager was startling. His eyes went wide and his hand shook a little. Allenby didn't notice or pretended not to. "You are doing very well. Now, this Madelaine, the dark pretty one, what did she say?"

"I don't remember that."

"Think!"

Ranse noticed that little specks of sweat were collecting around Parson's eyes. "Something about the cheque, I suppose. Or she may have just shown it to me."

"You were sitting where you are now. She came through that door from behind the counter. You looked up at her. Did she do anything?"

"Do?"

"Think hard. She's standing there. Did she look out the window onto the street, for instance?"

"Yes, yes, that's right. She did. But there's nothing to that. All the girls do it. You've done it yourself, a couple of times, as people go past."

"Indeed. But did she look in any different way? With more intensity, for instance, as though perhaps looking for someone?"

The manager thought hard. Ranse could almost hear

150

the machinery ticking. "Well, yes, come to think of it, she did stare rather hard."

"At somebody on the sidewalk right here, or perhaps across the street?"

Parsons wrinkled his brow again. "Look, I don't think it meant anything, but I do remember now that she seemed to be looking across the street, where the cars are parked."

"Good man. Very well. It is now two minutes to three. You are sitting here at your desk, alone, still going over the loan application. What did you do?"

"Well, I looked at my watch and then I started to get up to go and lock the front door, as I always do, and he came in."

"Which door?"

"Why, that one beside you, the one that leads into the rotunda of the bank."

"I see. Now this is the important part. All the rest has just been a warm-up. Keep your mind on his entrance. He came in. What did he look like?"

Parsons sighed with relief and spread his hands out. "This is the easy part. I've been over it so many times. He had on overalls, coveralls, a beat-up hat. Dark glasses. He was clean-shaven, with a scar on his cheek. And he had a gun." The manager beamed like a kid in school who has got all his answers right.

"Very good. Those are the obvious things. The things he wanted you to notice. How tall was he?"

"Well, would you mind standing for a minute? You too, Ranse?"

Both men stood. Allenby was about six feet three, Ranse about five eleven.

The manager surveyed them carefully. "Not as tall as either of you."

"Much shorter?"

"Than you, yes. Couple of inches shorter than Ranse."

"Was he standing straight or stooped over?"

"Kind of stooped over. I noticed that."

"So, he might well have been taller than he looked."

"Yes, he might have been."

"Now think. Was he purposely stooped, or was that his natural posture?"

"What?"

"It's important."

"Gosh. When a man's pointing a gun at you, you don't much care if he's on his hands and knees." The manager laughed, but Allenby didn't.

"You may have noticed more than you think."

Parsons screwed up his face. "Well, yeah, he did look kind of funny."

"As though he were wearing a theatrical costume perhaps."

"Yeah. Like a man dressed up as a hayseed."

"Good man. Now, the hat. Describe it."

"An old felt hat with the brim turned down."

"Good. And the hair. Real or a wig?"

Now Ranse was beginning to sweat himself, just a little under the arms.

"The hair. The hair. Gosh, the hair. It sort of stuck out. Yes, yes." Now he was excited. "It could have been a wig! Well, what do you know?"

"And his complexion. Was he tanned?"

"Yes, yes, very tanned. Everybody is here."

"Now think. A farmer is tanned differently from a tourist. He's more burnt."

"No, he was tanned."

"Could it have been theatrical makeup, do you think?"

Ranse held himself under control. Josie. Had she told this man about his acting career? Probably had. She told everybody. As though she wanted to show that her husband was more than just a dumb gumshoe. A man of culture.

The manager was thinking hard. "No, no, I don't think so. I'd have noticed. I've been in plays myself, you know. Remember *Arsenic and Old Lace*, Ranse, that you directed for us last year?"

Allenby's eyes flicked towards Ranse, but Ranse's face told him nothing.

"Yeah, I remember. Especially you falling into the

window seat in the dark and almost putting your back out."

Parsons laughed loudly with relief.

Allenby waited, and then asked, "Now the gun. What did you notice about it?"

"I'm afraid I know nothing about hand guns. Shotguns, yes. Or deer rifles."

"Was it an automatic or a revolver?"

"What's the difference?"

"An automatic has the shells in the handle in a clip. A revolver has a revolving chamber that holds six bullets."

"Like a six-shooter."

"Correct. Only much smaller."

Now the manager was really thinking and Ranse held his breath.

"Gosh. It was black."

"Good." Allenby waited.

"I'm sorry, but I can't say. I think his hand hid most of the gun."

"Very well. Did it strike you that he was a man used to guns?"

"What do you mean?"

"The way he handled it?"

Again the manager thought. "I don't know. He had it in his hand and it was pointed at me and . . . ."

"Was his hand shaking?"

"No, no, steady as a rock. I was the one shaking!" Again the nervous laugh.

"Natural enough. What did he say to you?"

Step by step, detail after detail, Allenby took Parsons through the rest of the holdup, all the time dragging out of his reluctant mind little details that he'd never mentioned before. The big clock on the wall ticked its way past eleven, and then past twelve.

When they got to the part about the shot being fired, Allenby asked: "Show me where the bullet hit."

"What?"

"Where it hit. He fired. The bullet went somewhere. In the wall perhaps?"

"Oh, that. Well, they never found it. The OPP searched

everywhere, but no sign of it. The robber aimed right over the young man's head, but the bullet just disappeared."

Allenby didn't go and look at the wall. He merely shook his head. "Obviously a blank. I thought it would be."

"Why a blank?"

"Our friend didn't want to run the risk of shooting anybody. Very wise to use blanks. Never can tell what one will do in a moment of crisis. One thing more."

"Yes?"

"Why is that night-lock chain on the front door?"

"Why? Well, it makes it easier to lock out the public when closing time comes."

"Without a key?"

"Yes. More convenient that way."

"Especially for a robber. I've noticed it in other branches. I shall recommend that the door be locked only with a key. No night-latches or chains. Well, that's all. Many thanks."

"I'm afraid I haven't told you much."

"You've told us a great deal. More than you realize. And I've kept you long enough. I shall be around for a few days, if you happen to think of anything else. Contact me or Mr. McGruber."

"Okay."

"And you realize, of course, that it is of the utmost importance that you talk to no one about this. Not one word. I'm sure our man is local. Probably still here in town. We can't have him getting the wind up."

"Don't worry, I won't tell a soul. Somebody in town. Wow! That's going to be tough for you, Ranse."

"Perhaps. In any case, I repeat. Don't discuss any aspect of the case with anyone. Not your staff, not anyone. So far as you're concerned, you can forget the whole thing."

"Not very likely. But I know enough not to talk about it."

"Good. Now, if you don't mind, I'd like to discuss a few things with Mr. McGruber. Privately."

When Parsons had gone, Allenby stood at a window looking at the street not more than a foot away.

"Street full of people. Man runs out with a garbage bag chock full of money, and nobody sees him."

"Oh, somebody saw him!" Ranse said.

"Yes, I know. He got into a red car, a blue car, a black car, where an accomplice was waiting, and drove off down the street. Do you believe that?"

"No."

"What do you believe?"

"Maybe he didn't have a car on the main street. He could have parked it right behind the bank. Then he could have run down the lane beside the bank and pulled out onto the highway going west."

"Strange. That's the theory of our friend across the street. Tirp, is it?"

"Tip. Timothy, really. But everybody calls him Tip."

"Seems to know a lot about this robbery, our friend Tip. Might be worth checking him out. What do you think of the manager?"

"Lying in a couple of places."

"Yes, the cheque. He's probably having it on with the beautiful brunette, and she came in to bite his ear."

Ranse laughed. He was enjoying it. Just like old times. Working with a smart partner. And then he remembered the real facts of the case and he didn't enjoy it so much.

"I'll tell you what I've learned about Alec Parsons," Allenby said, checking his notebook, "Little old to be still in a small branch. He was a prisoner of war. Just a kid really, at the time. Eighteen or nineteen. Joined as soon as war broke out. Military family. Dunkirk. Spent the remainder of the war in prison camps."

"Wow! I never knew that."

"It affects them. He never got over it, really. Been in half a dozen branches. Good record. Somewhat given to drink. Worth watching."

"You suspect him? Having a part in it, I mean?"

"I suspect everybody. You know that. Well, I must be off. Good to get back into it?"

"Yes, rather." He'd never used that expression in his life. Old habit of imitating.

"Good man. Keep in touch. Your cheques will start arriving in about a week. Anything you want to know about anyone in the bank, phone me at the lodge." They shook hands and went out onto the street.

After Allenby had gone, Ranse walked to his own car. Parsons was sitting in it.

"Want to talk to you, Ranse," he said in a whisper. "Get in."

Ranse got in. "Yeah, what is it?"

"Boy, I don't know. Talk about your fine-tooth comb!" He was very agitated. "Ranse, I had nothing to do with this. You know that."

"Sure."

"Look, I know I haven't been any hotshot banker. But I'm honest, goddamnit. I'm honest!"

"I believe you are."

"But I think I know who might be mixed up in it."

"Yeah?"

"Madelaine. Now just a minute. She's been seeing a lot of a new guy in town. A Jerry." The way he said it, Ranse could feel the hatred. "One of those lean, hard, blonde bastards. Why the hell we ever let so many of those people into the country, I don't know! Our guys get killed fighting them, and then they come over here and get good jobs. Why, do you know . . . ?"

"I know, Alec. What about him?"

"Well, I've seen him a few times with Madelaine. Younger than she is, too. Sometimes a girl will do anything for a guy. Especially a jock like that. All muscle and, Jesus, I don't know how they can stand them! Drives a sports car and acts as though he owns the world."

"The young do own the world, Alec. You know that."

"Well, I don't trust him. Nor her neither."

"Is that just a prejudice, or have you got something to go on?"

"Oh, I've got something to go on, all right."

"What?"

"I'll tell you later when I'm more sure. I'll see you, Ranse."

He got out of the car and walked off down the street towards his house.

Ranse drove home.

CHAPTER SEVENTEEN

"Mom, what's the matter?" Susie asked.

Susie and her family had arrived about ten o'clock from the city to spend the weekend. Their excuse was that the fall colour season was beginning. The leaves of the oaks, maples, sumacs, beeches and other trees were putting on a gorgeous show of colour, but they would not reach their climax until about October first, after which the leaves would gradually shrivel and drop.

It was a time when Torontonians swarmed to Muskoka in cars, special buses, and special trains to see the colours. They would be followed by the hunters, and the woods would be full of men with shotguns and rifles, seeking partridge and deer. They in turn would be followed by the snowmobilers, and the woods would be polluted by the roar of two-cycle motors and the stench of gas fumes.

But early September was the quiet season.

Susie and Josie were in the kitchen, which looked out onto three large sumacs whose leaves were already flaming red. Josie glanced at her daughter.

"What makes you think there is anything wrong?" she asked.

"You're worried, Mom, I can see it. Well, maybe not so much worried as preoccupied."

Josie laughed. "No, I'm not. Happy in fact, especially today with you and the children here."

"And you are doing a nice job of evading the question."

"No, really."

"How did you find Dad when you came home?"

"Why, the same as usual."

"Not preoccupied, absent-minded? I thought he seemed that way at the airport."

"Oh, you did? Well, my dear, you must face the fact that your parents are getting old."

"Mother."

"Oh, yes, it happens, you know. I remember when I first realized that my own folks were getting on. They were about our age."

"But you're both so healthy. And Dad–"

"Oh, I know. He jogs and swims and builds things like a young man. But he's sixty-one years old. And that makes a difference. I have to remember that, too."

"In what way?"

Josie was remembering. "Always when we've been separated for any length of time, the first thing he'd do was pick me up and carry me into the bedroom."

"Mother!"

"What's the matter?"

"Well, really."

"Does it shock you to realize that your old fogey parents still enjoy sex?"

"No, no, of course not. It's just, well, I've never heard you talk this way before."

"You've never brought up the subject before."

"Mother, you've changed."

"Oh, yes. You see, I've gotten older, too. And maybe, just maybe, like you and other females of today, I'm becoming liberated."

This was a bit much for Susie but before she could think of anything to say, her mother continued. "Oh, yes. You have no idea the restrictions we grew up with in the Methodist Church, or anywhere else, for that matter. Especially, we never talked about sex. Do you know that when you were coming, I didn't even know how babies were born?"

"But, surely, your mother–"

"A wonderful woman. And a hide-bound, prim, prissy woman, too. She would never talk to her daughter about sex. Any more, of course, than to warn us not to 'lose our reputation.' Once you did that you were finished."

"Like a heroine of a Thomas Hardy novel."

"Exactly. Women were put upon by men–if they weren't careful. The idea of sex being a mutually gratifying experience, well, nice girls certainly didn't think so!"

"But how did you overcome all that?"

"I'm not sure I have, completely, but I'm trying."

Susie put her arm over her mother's shoulder and gave her a slight squeeze. She was thinking of the time she had answered the phone at the cottage while Ranse was away on his fishing trip. A woman's voice, a young woman. Who was she and what did she want?

Her thoughts were interrupted by the twins bursting through the door.

"Where's Ranse?" Tim asked. "Isn't he home yet?"

"You mean your grandfather?" It bothered Susie that both the boys called Ranse by his first name. He had encouraged it, warning that anyone who referred to him as Pop, or Gramps, or any other such cognomen would receive a stiff boot in the backside.

The boys ignored her tone. "But where the heck is he?"

"He's in town," Josie told them, "and he'll be back soon, I hope."

"I sure hope so, too. Come on, let's go see if we can find one." They were gone out the door.

When Ranse returned, he wasn't out of the car before they were on him.

"Ranse!" Patrick yelled. "Can we go and look for rattlesnakes?"

"Massasauga rattlers," Tim added.

Ranse got out of his car, tucked a boy under each arm and headed for the patio. "Well, well, you two little pigaloomers. What's this about snakes?"

Like most twins, they finished each other's sentences.

"Dad took us to the CNE last week."

"And the neatest place of all was the exhibit of the Department of Lands and Forests."

"Yeah. We saw a fox and a badger and a marten."

"And a raccoon and a skunk and all sorts of snakes. They were the best."

"Especially the massasauga rattler. The ranger said they are found around Georgian Bay."

"And when we asked him if there were any in Muskoka, he said maybe."

"That's right, Ranse! Have you seen one yet?"

"Matter of fact, I saw a dead one on the road about a week ago."

"Wow!"

"First I've ever seen in this area. Maybe out on Rattlesnake Island." As soon as he said it, he wished he hadn't. The trouble with living a lie.

"Gosh! Can we go and find one?"

"Yeah. A live one. Maybe we could catch it."

"What would you do with a rattlesnake?"

"Put him in a box and sort of study him. Find out what he eats–and stuff like that."

"Um, hmm. Well."

"When can we go?"

"Well."

"But we can go, can't we?"

"We'll see."

Patrick was thoughtful. "Why is it adults always say, 'we'll see'?"

"And why is it that, when they do, it usually means no?" Tim added.

"I don't know," Ranse said. "Maybe for the same reason kids are always asking to do things adults don't want to do."

"Why don't you want to go to Rattlesnake Island?"

Funny thing, Ranse thought, when he was planning this caper and trying to think of all the possible problems that might come up, he'd never once thought of the twins. Or the kids' parents. But everybody in his clan

161

was a problem, he realized. Impossible to do something dramatically different from what one always did without the clan at least wondering about it. But any further discussion of adult-child relationships was cut off by the arrival of another car in the driveway. Soon Alec Parsons appeared on to the patio.

"Well, hello, Alec," Ranse greeted him. "Have a chair, take the load off. What brings you out here on your day off?"

But Parsons didn't sit. He stood fidgeting and looked uncomfortable. "Ranse, can I talk to you? In private?"

"Of course." Ranse glanced at the twins.

"Okay, okay," Patrick said. "We're going. Okay if we go up on the rock wall and look for snakes?"

"Sure. Just be careful."

They disappeared down the path like a couple of deer.

"Sit down, sit down," Ranse said. "You make me nervous standing there, looking as though you were ready to cut and run."

"Maybe I ought to." Parsons sat down wearily.

"What are you talking about?"

"Ranse, why did you take this job to investigate the robbery?"

Ranse thought for a minute, decided to be frank. "The pay is good. And it is in my line of experience."

"Yeah, I suppose so. But you start asking a lot of questions around, and it might lead you up some paths you don't exactly want to go."

"I don't understand that."

Parsons got up from his chair, walked to the edge of the patio, stood looking at the lake for a moment, lit a cigarette and turned to Ranse.

"I suppose you know I was having an affair with Madelaine."

My God, Ranse thought, you, too! A twinge of something he hadn't felt in years jarred his mind. Jealousy. Good old-fashioned jealousy! Aloud he said, "No, I didn't know it. Didn't even think of it."

"Yeah. I guess nobody did. We always left town." He

rubbed his face unhappily. "It's over, of course, but I know that if she wiggled her little finger I'd be back."

Ranse was pondering the cliché. The mental picture of Madelaine wiggling her little finger, in the classic siren gesture, was bothering him. He, too, would come running, he knew.

Parsons rubbed his hand over his forehead and glanced towards the glass doors, but nobody was coming out. He moved his wooden chair close to Ranse's. "You know what happened to me during the war?"

"Just that you were a POW after Dunkirk."

"Yeah. And my girl. While I was away. Four years. She just couldn't wait. When I came back, I was so bitter about women in general that I didn't have anything to do with them. For thirty years," he mused, "I didn't have anything to do with women, not seriously, that is. Just worked at my job, turned my mind into a computer full of figures. But even at that, I never got anywhere in the bank. Big companies don't exactly trust guys with no wives." He paused and looked around. "Jesus, Ranse, but you're lucky. All this. A great wife and family. Grandchildren. I wonder if guys like you realize just how lucky you are."

Ranse had no comment on that. "Why are you telling me all this, Alec?"

"You'd find out anyway, and maybe get the wrong idea. If the bank found out about it, it would be damned awkward. The affair is over. Didn't amount to much. Last winter we took our holidays at the same time and went to Miami. Spent a lot of money." His mind was back in Miami. "It was wonderful!"

Ranse was thinking like a detective. The set-up was perfect. Bank manager needs money to support a love affair. Plans with an accomplice to rob his own bank. Wouldn't be too hard to pin this on Parsons, he knew. He also knew that he would never do it.

"And now that damned German guy has got her. You know, Ranse, when I was a POW being kicked around by those bastards, I used to think about what we would do to

Germans after the war. But I never figured we'd hand over half our country to them. If I were you, I'd check up on that guy!''

"I will,'' Ranse assured him. "But it will make things easier if you keep your suspicions to yourself.''

"Don't worry!'' Shortly after that, he got up and left. Ranse watched him go, pondering, as he often had in the past, the whims of fate that got people into messes like that.

In town, Zeke parked his car in front of the drugstore, and went in to get some film for Susie. Sitting at the coffee counter at the back, he noticed a familiar figure in the uniform of the OPP. He went up to him and put a hand on his shoulder.

"Arnold. Arnold Grozenski. What are you doing here?''

The constable swivelled his stool. "Zeke! I work here. Part of our territory. What are you doing here?''

"Visiting the wife's folks, out at Wigwam Lake. Maybe you know my father-in-law, Ranse McGruber?''

"The retired detective? Sure. Sit down. I'll buy you a cup of coffee.''

"Okay.''

Tip Tipton came behind the counter. "Hi, Zeke,'' he said. "Cream and sugar?''

"Black, please.'' He turned to his friend. "Well, I heard you'd joined the Provincials. How is it going?''

"Not bad. Chasing crazy drivers on the highway, pinching people for not wearing seat belts, you know.''

"And investigating bank robberies, don't forget that,'' Tipton put in, setting the coffee in front of Zeke.

"Yeah. How about that?'' Zeke asked.

"Nothing's broken yet. Crazy thing. I was here shortly after it happened. Matter of fact, I met Mr. McGruber leaving town.''

"Oh?''

"Yeah. We set up a road block just at the end of town there. He was one of our first customers.''

"Yeah, I heard he'd been in town.''

"Right there in front of the bank, helping direct traffic," Tipton added. "Arrived on the scene just after the robber left."

"Did you see the robber leave?" Zeke asked.

"I saw a car drive away in a hurry. Green car that had been parked over on this side. Must have had an accomplice inside."

He turned around to pour some more coffee and the constable winked ever so slightly at Zeke, a wink that said: amateur detectives.

"I wonder what he was doing in town?" Zeke said, half to himself.

"Same as you or anybody else," Tipton told him. "Getting his mail or groceries, stuff like that."

"Yeah." Zeke turned the conversation to mutual friends, finished his coffee, got the film and left.

He walked across the street and stood in front of the bank for a minute, then went down the alleyway beside the bank, crossed the rutted land there, found the path through the woods, and walked along its winding course to see where it led. When he got to the liquor-store parking lot, he stood for a moment, looking back at the path, then walked across the lot to the highway and along it to the main street. He got into his car and drove back to the lake.

About four o'clock that afternoon, Zeke and Ranse went for a jog down Shorebank Road. Even though it was a weekend, they met practically no cars.

"So how's it going in the big city?" Ranse asked.

"Quiet. All the excitement seems to be out here."

"You mean our famous bank robbery. Pretty well forgotten around here."

"Suppose so. Ran into Arnold Grozenski in town. Says they haven't any new leads."

"That a fact?" Ranse wondered if the fact that he was on the case had become common knowledge yet. It would soon enough, he knew.

"You got any theories?" Zeke asked.

"None."

"Arnold said he met you that day, going out of town."

"I guess he met a lot of people."

"Did he search your car?"

"What?"

"Well, I just wondered what the attitude of one cop is to another."

"I suppose he did. I don't remember, exactly. I know he stopped me."

"Yeah."

They jogged along, side by side, in silence, each with his own thoughts.

Suddenly Zeke blurted out: "Say, did you know there's a path through the woods behind the bank?"

Ranse stopped, and after jogging a few steps farther, Zeke stopped and came back to him. "No, I didn't know that," Ranse said carefully. "But it's logical. Wherever there's a bush, kids make a path through it."

"This looks like an old one. Not used much. Very dark and secluded in there."

"You followed it?"

"Yeah. Comes out right at the liquor-store parking lot." Zeke was becoming animated. "Thief could have parked his car down there, robbed the bank, run back down the path, got in his car, and headed west out of town. Be miles away before anybody set up a road block. Could have got off the highway and gone up the Peninsula Road or south along the lake, or anywhere. Never find him on those winding roads. What do you think?"

"Possible. Very possible. As you say, there are hundreds of out-of-the-way places along those roads. Great place to disappear."

"I bet that's what must have happened."

Zeke had another theory, too. What if the thief had driven east instead of west, back up to the main street and joined in the confusion. But, of course, he'd have been recognized. Unless . . . .

They kept on jogging until they reached the bridge over the river, and then turned around and jogged back. The road was still empty.

As Susie and Zeke were getting ready for bed that night in the small bedroom facing the lake, Susie was in a kittenish mood. She snapped the elastic on the top of Zeke's pajamas.

"Hey, we're on a holiday," she teased.

"Yeah, great," Zeke replied, without enthusiasm.

"And the twins are sound asleep in Dad's office."

"Office? Why does he call it an office?"

"Well, you know. Dad always wanted to write plays for television and he thought when he retired . . . ."

"What kind of plays?"

"Crime and punishment, I guess. The kind of thing he knows best. But who cares? We are here, man and woman; the moon is shining in through the window and shimmering on the lake and we're young and in love, and . . . ."

But something was gnawing at Zeke's mind. A detective's mind. A highly suspicious mind. The kind of mind that, like a porcupine, once it's begun to gnaw, keeps at it.

Susie knew this mind, but she had teased him out of such moods before. Maybe she could do it again. "Well, old sobersides, doesn't that moon do anything to you?"

"Your dad," Zeke said. "When you phoned him, over a month ago when Josie was away, what did he say?"

"I haven't the slightest idea what you are talking about."

"The weekend after the holdup at the bank. Remember? We came up here, and Ranse was away on his fishing trip."

"Yes, sir, you have got your facts exactly right!"

"Well, what did he sound like when you talked to him on the phone?"

"What in the world are you getting at?"

"Jumpy or nervous?"

"Zeke! Are you trying to connect my father . . . my father with that bank holdup?"

Zeke scratched his head in discomfort. "I don't know. Of course not! But, well, I discovered something today that—"

"Oh, no. Your nasty little suspicious mind is at work, I see, and about my father!" She was furious, sitting there in her flimsy nightgown. Furious not so much at what had happened or been said, as at what had not happened.

"There's some funny aspects to this case. I ran into Arnold Grozenski in the drugstore."

"You mean Arnold Grozenski, the Ontario Provincial Police constable?"

"Yeah. You remember him?"

"I'll not listen to any more of this. I simply won't do it!" She snatched up her robe, threw it over her shoulders, and started for the door.

"Where are you going?"

"To the living room to read a book. Probably a Harlequin Romance!"

In the bedroom down the hall, Josie lay on her side beside Ranse. She gently laid her hand on his thigh, but there was no response. He seemed to be asleep. So she turned over and tried to go to sleep herself.

But Ranse wasn't asleep. Had to keep his head clear. Next week he would begin his investigations of the robbery by talking to some members of the staff. And one of the first people he would talk to, he decided, was Madelaine. The thought of her kept him awake even after his wife fell asleep.

CHAPTER EIGHTEEN

Monday morning Ranse McGruber awoke at six o'clock and he knew from experience that he wouldn't go back to sleep. Besides, he'd always liked getting up early and having breakfast alone. A time to himself, a time to do some thinking. He'd listen to the CBC morning news and interview show. Keep my normal schedules, he thought.

He closed the bedroom door carefully so as not to awaken Josie, and moved the radio over near the stove where he was cooking his egg and making the toast.

The police situation in Toronto was still hot. The mayor wanted an independent board to review police actions; the police commissioner was dead against it. Same old thing, Ranse thought, people hollering about law and order and crime, but as soon as the police do something forthright they're onto them. Oh well, a policeman's lot is not an easy one.

The economy still in a mess. Price of gold well over the four hundred mark. American dollar in trouble; Canadian dollar in bigger trouble. And he had a couple hundred thousand of them hidden under a rock. The irony of it made Ranse grimace with frustration. Poor little rich boy!

Then the six-thirty news. A whole family bludgeoned to death in a fashionable suburb. No clues, no apparent motive. Looked like a hit man, Ranse thought. Somebody the family evidently knew, the item said. No sign of a break-in or a struggle; nothing stolen. The toughest kind of case to crack.

Traffic in Toronto: bad. Tractor-trailer jackknifed on a ramp. Don Valley Parkway plugged. Report on Expo game. Wouldn't it be something if the World Series were played in Montreal? Didn't look as though it would ever be played in Toronto.

Then a song by his one-time favourite female vocalist. Ranse grimaced with distaste. She had ceased to be his favourite singer after he'd seen her a thousand times on television singing the praises of a bank. Same with his favourite Canadian comedians, who used to break him up but who had lost their appeal when they started selling automobile tires. Greed, he thought, ruined by greed.

As he was pouring boiling water into the teapot, an item caught his ear that interested him. A policewoman who worked the street in the area north of Wellesley and east of Jarvis. His old beat. More prostitutes to the block than anywhere else in Canada. He'd known some of the women well; one or two of them too well.

The policewoman explained how she went out on the street at night with a back-up car nearby, and was propositioned by men whom the team subsequently arrested.

"What kind of men?" the interviewer asked.

"All kinds. Businessmen, lawyers, doctors, stockbrokers, the man next door."

"What was their reaction when arrested?"

"Shock. And disbelief. Some of them said they didn't think men could be arrested for soliciting, just women. Mostly they were afraid of the publicity. That their wives would find out."

"Did you form any opinion about why they were there?"

"Well, it's hard to explain. Obviously, they were looking for something they weren't getting at home. A new sexual experience. Excitement. Little-boy naughtiness. Doing something on the sly with nobody knowing. And the fact that underneath the exterior of everyone there is another person whose desires, hang ups, fantasies, needs can't even be guessed at."

"That's interesting. Like the 'respectable citizen' who

kidnapped a twelve-year-old girl and kept her in a cave under the front porch of his house."

"That's right. And then there's another reason why men seek prostitutes. Fear."

"Fear?"

"Fear of failure. There's so much talk these days about female orgasms, and of how many wives are left unsatisfied, that husbands can become afraid they won't give their wives what they want. With a prostitute, they know what she wants–money. And that they can give."

Money, Ranse thought. Indeed the root of all evil. He remembered as a boy of twelve he'd read *Treasure Island*, and how it had come as a shock to him that these characters would do anything for money. Long John Silver, such a nice, pleasant, friendly man. Ranse could still feel the horror of the moment when Long John hurled his crutch at one of the pirates who had crossed him, hitting him in the back and knocking him down, and then sprang forward on his one leg to plunge his knife into the pirate's back. Like Jim Hawkins, young Ranse McGruber had, for the first time, realized the power of greed. And he shuddered to realize it.

And most of the other stories he'd read had the same theme. Pirates of the Spanish Main killing for gold. Pieces of eight. And he remembered a story in *Chums* titled "Gold: a Mystery," wherein a professor discovered the secret of how to turn lead into gold, and the scheming and deceit and murder that resulted from this discovery.

Money and sex, the two things for which men would lie and steal and kill. *La belle Dame sans Merci hath thee in thrall.*

Which naturally made him think of Madelaine and the interview he would have with her later that week. Was she la belle dame? No bloody doubt but that she had him in thrall. And like that poor knight "alone and palely loitering," he was helpless to do anything about it. Even now, alone in his own kitchen, munching toast and honey and drinking strong tea, with his wife of thirty-six years stirring in the bedroom, he felt himself aroused by

171

the thought of smooth, tanned skin and delectable breasts.

And there was danger there, too. He knew it.

When Josie came out into the living room, her hair was combed, and she was fully dressed in an attractive housecoat. He marvelled at her anew. Never slouching about the house in some shabby get-up with curlers in her hair. In all their years together, she had managed, somehow, through having children and back trouble and arthritis in her hands, to look trim and attractive.

And he could tell–after years you can always tell–that she was concerned and worried about him. He knew she wouldn't ask, or nag, or even suggest that anything was wrong. She came over to where he was sitting and gave him a light kiss on the forehead. An understanding kiss. And somehow he resented that kiss. It was like the kind pat on the head one would give to a faithful dog.

She poured herself some tea. "What are your plans for today?" she asked.

"Plans? No plans. Butt about the house. Fix that gas line in the boat. Got to go in to town this afternoon."

"Detective work?"

"Yeah. Kind of."

She said no more. He knew she was dying to ask him if he had any suspicions about the robbery, and he knew she wouldn't do it. Long ago, she had learned that his professional life and his home life were entirely separate, and that he didn't talk about one when involved with the other.

But Josie didn't say anything. No comments on how beautiful it was, or how peaceful or about how lucky they were to have such a gorgeous place. She just sat there beside him and stared out through the glass doors at the riot of colour in the trees and said nothing. This was bad. For Ranse knew that when Josie was silent she was worried or sad or unhappy. He tried to think of something to say, but what can you say to a spouse whom you are deceiving, lying to and thinking seriously about leaving?

The phone rang.

"You get that," Ranse said. "Probably one of your

ladies, and I don't feel like exchanging pleasantries with them just now."

Josie went to the little pine table Ranse had built for the phone.

"Hello?"

Ranse was always intrigued by Josie's side of a phone conversation. She could talk and exclaim and shout with laughter and gasp with horror, and then when he asked her what was wrong, she'd say, "Oh, nothing. You know Susie."

But now she did none of those things. "Why, hello, Mr. Allenby," she said in her most cheerful, pleased voice. "Why I'm just fine. It's such a beautiful day. Oh, imagine that." And then she laughed her warm, intimate laugh. "What a nice thing to say! Ranse is right here. Do you want to talk with him?"

Ranse half rose from his chair. Allenby. Now what in hell did he want at this hour of the morning? Was he going to be a pest who phoned every day?

But Josie wasn't coming off the phone. "This afternoon? Well, it certainly is a lovely day for it. But I don't know. I'll have to ask Ranse. Here, I'll let you speak to him."

She handed Ranse the phone, with her hand over the mouthpiece. "He wants us to go on a boat cruise. Somebody gave him three tickets."

"What?" Into the phone he said, "Hello, Mr. Allenby."

"Yes. Well, look, old man, I'm sorry to bother you this early, but, as I was telling your charming wife, this has to be arranged this morning."

"What does?"

"Well, this may sound frightfully impulsive, but there's a most delightful cruise that leaves the lodge here at two this afternoon and comes back at dusk. Goes right through the whole lake system. Dinner and all that. I was wondering if you and your wife would join me."

"A boat cruise?" Ranse was trying to figure out what this was all about.

"Yes. May not get another day like this for some time.

I think it might be rather good fun. That is, of course, if you haven't anything urgent on for this afternoon?"

"Well, as a matter of fact, I do have."

"Oh." There was real disappointment in his voice. "Well, perhaps your wife would like to go with me."

"Yes. She might like that. Look, I'll ask her. She'll call you back."

"Fine. I'll be here. You have the number. Er, I hope you don't mind my suggesting that?"

"Not at all."

Ranse hung up the phone and turned to his wife. It seemed to him that she was more animated and younger looking. "Well, I'm damned."

"You told him you couldn't go."

"Yes. And he wanted to know if you could go."

"Oh, no, I wouldn't do that!"

"Why not? This cove seems to have a bit of a crush on you, don't you know."

"Me?" She was actually blushing. "An old grandmother like me!"

"A damned attractive grandmother." But he wasn't thinking of her attractions. Rather of the attractions of another. Something else was bothering him. "I wonder what Allenby is up to?" he said, half to himself.

"Up to? Why, I think it's charming of him to invite us."

"Chahmin! Oh yes, indeed. Most frightfully chahmin!"

He considered his imitation to be pretty good, but Josie was not amused. "Ranse!" Her face was flushed with anger. "What's the matter with you?"

"With me? Nothing at all."

"You're acting so, well, so mean!"

He had that feeling that the thing was developing too far, but he couldn't stop. "Mean? No. I just think that you and Allenby hit it off pretty well on the aircraft; maybe you'd like to–"

"Like to what?"

Josie was angrier than he'd seen her in a long time. He

knew he'd better back off. He smiled his best smile. "I only mean that it might be okay. We've never been on one of these cruises, and they say they are fun. You might enjoy it."

"Do you want me to go?" Her lips were a straight line.

"Sure. If you want to. Look, it's no big deal. I'll be busy most of the afternoon. I'll drive you over there. It's a beautiful day. Sure, I think you should go."

"Then I will."

"Look, there's nothing to be upset about."

"Who's upset?" Josie went back to the phone and made her call. "He's going to pick me up in his car. So you won't have to drive me over to the lodge after all."

"Okay. Fine." The whole thing had taken on an unreality that Ranse couldn't quite fathom. As though he were reading lines in a play. And the script of this play, he realized, had bogged down. It wasn't moving. He would have to do something and soon. Something decisive. Get the money from Rattlesnake Island. That wouldn't be difficult, but what to do with it? Where to go? And with whom?

The scenario, he knew, was writing itself in his mind, and, like a character in a play, he had no control over its outcome. That's the way it was written; that's the way it would be. From a play-writing book that he'd studied assiduously, he knew the essential steps in a drama. They were the Preparation, Attack, Development, Turn and Outcome. Well, he'd certainly been through the Preparation part, with the beard and all. And the Attack, when he'd actually robbed the bank and set up the essential problem of the drama. The Development had moved along, with complications, suspense, incident; and now it was time for the Turn. Or the Climax. Rising action to the climax. That was it.

Somehow, he knew that his talk with Madelaine would be the Turn. And the Outcome would depend upon that Turn.

CHAPTER NINETEEN

As Josie sat on the patio waiting for her date to come and pick her up, she felt something of the excitement of her youth. She was glad Ranse wasn't there. He'd gone down to the shore to work on the boat, he said. Get it ready for winter.

Josie had put on a light print summer dress. It was warm for September, but since she knew it might be cool before she got home, she had a soft white shawl hanging on the back of the chair to take with her. She stretched out her bare legs in front of her and admired them. Still good legs. No ruptured veins. Good legs for a woman of nearing sixty.

Sixty! She'd always thought of women who reached the age of sixty as being over the hill, finished with life, content to knit sweaters for grandchildren. Calm, complacent, wise, and, above all, contented. Josie felt none of these things yet.

She was waiting for her date. Unlike her husband, Josie was not a schemer and a plotter. She tended to take things pretty much as they came and not to worry about what might happen or whether or not she should be doing what she was doing. Her heart ruled her mind. Heart, nonsense! It was hormones. She'd been gifted, or cursed, with a goodly supply of female hormones. She had always liked men and she still liked them. Women's liberation meant little to her. Oh, she was in favour of equal rights for women, but mostly because she was against injustice in any form. But this business of women being the adversaries of men had no meaning for her. Men and women cooperated, complemented each other, loved each other. Most of all in her life, Josie wanted love. And, for thirty-six years, she had had it from Ranse, a good man, a true man. But in her heart she knew that if he ever betrayed her, all that love and devotion could turn to hatred.

There had been occasions throughout her marriage when she had been tempted, when she had temporarily "fallen for" other men. Young men and older men. She had always been so open and fun-loving. And, yes, she had to admit it, something of a flirt. And it had happened at parties, usually when she was dancing–Josie loved to dance–that some man would make a pass and she would respond.

Often they would tell her that she was the kind of woman they'd been seeking all their lives. A "real woman" as some of them had put it, a woman who enjoyed life, who was kind and loving and generous. They always stressed the "generous" part.

And under the influence of gin and tonic, she had necked in dark corners and given warm, soft kisses. But she never went any farther. Partly it was her strong Methodist upbringing (nice girls didn't), but, more, it was her powerful love for Ranse. After such encounters she would be more passionate even than usual, and Ranse, who usually had been doing some flirting of his own, would respond–magnificently.

She looked up. There, coming up the patio steps, was James Allenby. Looking most awfully trim and neat he was, with a pair of grey slacks and an expensive sports shirt. David Niven to a T.

"Well," he said. "Don't you look smashing!"

Josie merely smiled her approval, got up from her chair and took his extended hand. She almost leaned forward to kiss him, but then realized that she hadn't known him long enough for that. Only good friends kissed when meeting.

"I say," Allenby went on, taking her hand gently in his large strong one, "it's most awfully decent of you to accept my invitation. Sorry Ranse couldn't make it. Are you sure he doesn't mind?"

"No, I'm not sure. I think I'd be disappointed if he didn't mind just a little. But I thank you for inviting us. I've never been on one of these cruises."

"Nor has anyone been on this one. It's the maiden voyage for the reconditioned *Neapuchin*. Seems she was once queen of the lakes."

"Yes, I've read about the lake steamers that took people on outings and, in fact, delivered them to their cottages."

"Exactly. Seems they've been reconditioning this old girl at great expense for two years now and they've finally got her ready. Tremendous excitement and promotion."

"I know. I hope she doesn't sink like the *Mariposa Belle*."

"What? Oh, you mean the cruise ship in Leacock's story." He laughed heartily.

"You know Leacock?"

"Everyone knows Leacock. I really think he was more popular in England in the twenties and thirties then he was over here."

"Probably. Shall we go?"

"Your husband? Don't you want to tell him we're leaving?"

"He knows. Probably out fishing by now."

"Oh. Well, shall we be off? Don't want to miss the grand launching."

Later, as they sat on the deck of the *Neapuchin* looking at the rocky, pine- and birch-covered shore slip by and listening to the strains of "Strolling Down the River" on the ship's gramaphone, Josie breathed a sigh of contentment. "Isn't this heavenly!"

"Indeed it is. Josie, I have a confession."

"A confession?"

"Oh, yes, indeed. You see, I wasn't given three tickets to this joy ride. I bought them."

"Why? I mean apart from enjoying our sparkling company?"

"I don't know. I really don't. An impulse."

"A hunch?"

"What? Oh, no, nothing like that. It's just that, well, my life is filled with suspicion, chicanery and, meeting you two such really nice people . . . ."

"And here I thought you brought me out here to have your wicked way with me."

He burst into loud, happy laughter. "My God, I haven't laughed like that in months! Not since Pamela died."

Involuntarily she reached over and placed her hand on his. "What was she like?"

"She was such a fine, loving woman." He straightened up. "You know, you're the first person I've really wanted to talk to about her."

"Where did you meet her?"

"During the war. She was a secretary in the Home Office. I was very young, and very eager, just the kind of chap the service needed, they said."

"Tell me about her."

"A bit on the tall side, taller than you. Brown hair, brown eyes. But, oh damn, it was none of those things that made me love her. How can you describe the essence of a person? She was, well, lovable. We were very happy for thirty years."

A man who can mourn so, for a woman with whom he's lived for thirty years, that is a loving man, Josie thought. Would Ranse mourn so for her? She hoped he would.

"Children?" she asked.

"Pamela couldn't have children. But somehow it didn't seem to matter. We had each other, you know?"

"I can't imagine my life without the children."

"Yes, you told me on the aircraft how much they meant to you. The old twins and the new ones."

"They are our grandchildren."

"Of course. And you?" he asked. "How did you come to marry a detective, a trusting person like you?"

"I fell in love. He swept me off my feet. I was engaged to a professor when I met Ranse–well, practically engaged–but he just wasn't the sweeping type."

"I see. What was he like, this non-sweeper?"

"Very nice. We used to go to the symphony concerts together. I loved them. And we had other intellectual pursuits."

"You were an intellectual?"

"Oh, I didn't know what I was. I went to the University of Toronto, and was a devotee of Bernard Shaw and Bertrand Russell, and became a socialist and an atheist in turn. The forties were a great time for both."

"But you outgrew both?"

"Heavens, no. I still hate all the rotten things that go on in this world. There seems no justice, the rich still get richer and the poor still get poorer. But I don't let myself dwell on it. That's an advantage women have, especially women with children and grandchildren."

"Yes, I suppose so. Don't you worry about, you know, after-life?"

"Nope. If there is, there is; if there isn't . . . well. Ranse says that I'm one person he knows who would go to heaven if there were a heaven."

"He's probably right. So, you found the policeman more interesting than the intellectual."

"Oh, Ranse is no dolt. He really knows a lot about drama. And he was a good actor. I always thought he could have been another Humphrey Bogart, if he'd had the chance."

Allenby didn't reply to this immediately. He seemed to be thinking of something. Then he muttered, "Yes, you told me about that on the plane."

"I must have told you a lot on that plane ride when you were plying me with drinks. Ranse says I tell everybody everything."

"That's because you trust people. It must be nice to trust people."

"Don't you?"

"I try to. But, you see, I was trained to trust nobody."

"How terrible. Ranse is the same. Sometimes I think he doesn't always trust me."

"I do. Somehow I think I trust you completely."

"Be careful. I might be stringing you a line."

"Stringing me–?"

Her laugh cut him short. "Oh, I see, you were having me on there." Then, seriously: "But I do think it important that we trust each other."

She felt a small chill of apprehension. "Is there something wrong?"

"I don't know. I'm not sure. I have this feeling that I can't shake and I wish I could." He turned to her and took her hand. "I want you to promise me something."

"Promise?"

"Oh, I know we haven't known each other very long, but I feel somehow that I have known you for a long time. Please, if anything should go wrong–with anything–will you get in touch with me, first?"

"But what could go wrong?"

"Nothing, I hope. Please promise."

"Well, all right, but I wish you'd tell me more."

"They've opened the bar. Can I get you something?"

"Oh, that would be nice. A gin and tonic, please."

He got up from his chair. "Gin and tonic. Right." He turned away, then paused and looked back. "With ice?"

"Of course."

"To be sure. Of course."

Then she remembered from the English officers she'd met during the war that they rarely had ice with their drinks. All those gallant young officers of wartime that she'd met in wardrooms! So attentive, so lonely, so always on the make. She hadn't thought of them in years. But now, on a pleasure cruise, it came back to her. The crazy war years. Nothing could ever be like them. Living for each day. Always on the move. Always meeting new and interesting people whom you'd never meet otherwise in a hundred years. Heady stuff. Fortunately, or unfortunately, she'd become pregnant and that put an end to some of the gaiety.

James Allenby came back with the drinks and they sat, side by side, sipping and thinking their own thoughts. Allenby's thoughts were of Ranse McGruber, but Josie's, strangely enough, weren't.

CHAPTER TWENTY

"What is wrong, darling?" Josie asked. They were sitting on the patio having their morning coffee. A hermit thrush sang in a nearby tree. As he listened, an old nursery rhyme rang through Ranse's head:

There's a merry brown thrush sitting up in a tree.
He's singing to you; he's singing to me.
And what does he say, little girl, little boy?
"Oh the world's running over with joy."

He'd forgotten the next part, but the last two lines were there:

"Don't meddle, don't touch, little girl, little boy,
Or the world will lose some of its joy."

He'd didn't realize it, but mumbled aloud: "Don't meddle, don't touch."

"What's that?" Josie asked.

"Huh?"

"What you just said."

"Nothing. Nothing. I'm sorry. Did you say something?"

"That's just it. Your mind seems somewhere else." She leaned towards him, face furrowed with concern.

"Ranse, there's something bothering you. I can tell."
Now that it was out, she kept on. "Ever since I came
home things have been, well, different."

"No . . . no . . . nothing's changed."

"Susie has noticed it, too. And Mr. Allenby-"

"Allenby!" It was a shout. "What about Allenby?"

"Something he said."

"What? What did he say?"

"It was strange. Something about letting him know if
anything happened."

"Happened? What could happen?"

"Ranse, darling, what *is* wrong?"

"Huh? Nothing. Just can't figure out why he'd say
that."

"Oh, I guess he was just being friendly. You know."

"I don't know. Goddamn it, that's just the point!"

"Why, Ranse! There's no reason to be angry."

"Sorry, sorry. Forget it. Must be this damned robbery
I'm working on. Poking into other people's business."

"Don't do it, Ranse. Phone James-"

"James?"

"Mr. Allenby, and tell him you can't do it. It's not
worth it."

"And give up three thousand? Maybe more? Not now."

"Why? Do you suspect somebody?"

He began to improvise. "Well, there's a young man.
He's been in town from about the time of the robbery.
Drives an expensive sports car. Has no job." He gathered
momentum. "Knew the bank. Friendly with one of the
bank girls, as a matter of fact."

Josie sighed. "So that's it. Well, dear, I am relieved."
But she wasn't, not really. She'd felt something was
wrong before he took on the investigation. And she had
never known her husband to act this way, even when he
was on the toughest case.

Ranse got up, leaving a half cup of coffee. "Got to go
down to the boathouse," he muttered, and went down
the path to the lake.

Willie! God, it would be easy to frame Willie for this
robbery. No. He'd never framed anybody in his entire

184

career. Well, not exactly framed. There was the deal he had with old Smokey, who hung around the drug people. Poor old Smokey.

But Willie. His rival. Dirty pool, somehow. Just the same, there was something fishy about that Kraut.

He heard the clanging of the metallic triangle they'd tied on a tree by the patio, the signal that Josie used to call him to the phone.

He went up the path.

"It's Alec Parsons," Josie said as he entered the house. "He sounds excited."

Ranse took the phone. "Alec?"

"Ranse!" He was excited. "Can you come into town right away? To the bank?"

"What's up?"

"I've got something I want to show you. Something damned important!"

A clue. Could Parsons have found something? But what? "Okay. I'll be there in three quarters of an hour."

When he walked into the bank, he glanced at Madelaine's wicket. She was talking to a customer and she looked excited and happy, far more excited and happy than that old coot she was talking to could make her feel.

Ranse went through the open door into Parson's office. The manager got out of his chair and closed both doors.

"Sit down."

Ranse sat. "What's up?"

"This is up." He picked up a newspaper clipping from his desk and handed it to Ranse. "Just read that."

Ranse took the paper and noted the date. Ten weeks ago. The headline said: RCMP BUST DOPE RING ON EAST COAST.

The story told of the capture of a power boat off Cape Breton Island, a boat loaded with marijuana and cocaine. Four men had been arrested.

"I think I saw this," Ranse said.

"And did you see the part where one of the men dived overboard in the dark and got away? They didn't know if he drowned or swam to shore?"

Ranse read on. The account pointed out that it was unlikely the suspect had made it to shore, unless he were an exceptional swimmer.

An exceptional swimmer!

Parsons was excited. "Who do we know that's an expert swimmer and arrived here not long after that?"

"Willie?"

"You've got it!" Parsons almost jumped out of his chair. "They tell me Columbia's crawling with those damned Nazis and their families. This is one of them and he's got into the drug trade. It all figures."

"He said he was a defector from East Germany."

"He did? When?"

Yes, when? "He tells everybody that. It's common knowledge."

"Oh. Well, he could have made that up. Just say you hate the Commies and everybody believes you. The bastards."

"I can check it out."

"How?"

"Phone Allenby. He's got connections in the RCMP."

"Do that, Ranse. I bet he's our bank robber. Just the right height and everything."

"Do you know where he lives?" Ranse asked.

"Yeah, at Mrs. Simpson's boarding house. You know the one."

"I know." Ranse folded the clipping. "Can I keep this for a while?"

"Yeah, sure. What are you going to do?"

What was he going to do? Ranse's mind was racing now. Willie a criminal. First of all, he had to make sure.

Somehow, through all this, he sensed a way out for him and Madelaine. Willie a criminal. People who rob banks are criminals, not respectable citizens, members of the Legion, devoted family men with a spotless record for honesty and integrity.

And when he thought of Willie, he thought of Madelaine. The picture of them together on his patio came into his mind. Willie and Madelaine. Two beautiful young people, obviously enamoured of each other. Enamoured–what the hell–lusting for each other.

Willie a criminal. Not just a defector, not just a possible spy or fifth columnist–that was Graham Greene stuff. This was real, the kind of thing he understood from his experience. So what does a detective do when he's hot on the heels of a possible suspect? He proceeds with care and precision. He builds up a case. Sometimes he manufactures a case. This had happened before now. But that's how you deal with criminals. They are fair game, you see; crime is their business, and your business is to apprehend them. So what if it takes a bit of manipulating here and there? They have many advantages. The law protects them. Sometimes you have to circumvent the law. Just a little bit.

But how?

Ranse left the bank and walked down the street and checked the boarding house. Willie's Porsche was parked outside. Keeping a watchful eye for any sign of his quarry, he headed for a pay phone.

Luckily, Allenby was at the lodge. He listened to what Ranse had to say.

"Schmitt, you say. Willie Schmitt. A defector? From a swimming team? When?"

Ranse told him. "Of course, that may not be his real name."

"Description?"

Ranse described Willie over the phone, and with every detail of his youthful, muscular, bronzed person, Ranse hated him more. "And an expert swimmer. That's important."

"And he's the friend of that young lady in the bank? I say, have you met this bloke?"

Have to be careful here. Caution always. "No, I've never actually met him, but he's the one Parsons mentioned. In the bank on Saturday."

"Yes, yes, of course. You think they may be in this together?"

Another angle. Madelaine in jeopardy. Like the Wren in the navy. He could save her and she would be grateful. "I'm not sure. Possibly. I'll talk to her after we know more about Willie."

"Perhaps I'd better talk to her."

"I'll handle it." There was an edge to Ranse's voice. "That's what you're paying me for."

"Just so. Well, I'll get on to Ottawa right away. Where can I reach you? At home?"

"No, I want to stay in town and keep an eye on things. The suspect lives in a boarding house just off the main street. His car is parked out in front. How long will it take you to find out?"

"Not long. I have a direct line, so to speak."

Ranse was thinking. "I'll be at the coffee bar in the drugstore. Here's the number. Hold on."

He manoeuvred the phone book up onto the little shelf under the phone and, holding the receiver cradled against his shoulder, found the number.

"Fine. I'll check with you there within the hour."

Ranse left the booth and walked down the main street, over the bridge, past the post office and down a side street. Willie's car was still there. Should he confront him now? Bluff him, maybe. If only he had some evidence. Anything! But all the evidence had been destroyed.

Except the rubber boots.

Plant them in Willie's car?

No, no, too dangerous. Somebody might see him, even at night. And Ranse had a feeling he had to work fast. This drama had reached its climax, and a new plan was forming in his mind. A plan that called for immediate action.

He went back and walked along the main street towards Tip Tipton's place. He looked over at the bank. Three thirty-six. The bank was closed. The staff would soon be leaving, and then Madelaine would go home. And Willie . . . .

Ranse went into the drugstore and back to the coffee

counter. Mayor Bradshaw was there and Tom Wilkinson. They moved over to give Ranse a seat on the end stool.

"Well, how's our gentleman of leisure?" the mayor asked.

"Must be nice to have nothing to do all day," Wilkinson added.

Ranse sat on the stool. "I don't notice you guys working your butts off."

Tip Tipton, who'd had his back to the counter while he poured a cup of coffee, turned around and set it before Ranse. "Besides," he winked at Ranse, "our friend here isn't a man of leisure any more."

"Oh? What you doing, Ranse?" the mayor asked.

Ranse looked hard at Tipton. "Oh, just the usual–fishing, shooting pool, darts. I tell you it's a busy life."

"I thought maybe you might have gone back into your old profession, temporarily," Wilkinson hinted, looking sideways at Ranse.

"Well there's somebody playing detective around here, only he ain't playing," Tipton said.

Ranse's radar was immediately sensitized.

"Who's that?" he asked, as casually as he could.

"Some English guy. Looks like that old movie actor."

"David Niven?"

"Yeah. That guy can ask more questions while drinking a cup of coffee. Oh, very casual like. But I'm onto him. Wanted to know all about what I saw and that. Very interested in you, too." Again the wink.

"Me?"

"Yeah. You know, how you showed up and directed traffic."

"What did he say about that?"

"Nothing. Just listened."

Tipton looked up over their heads and along the aisle of deodorants and headache pills, through the front window where he could see the bank across the street. "Bank staff leaving early. Caution how business just quits after the Summers go."

"Yeah," the mayor added. "Won't be much happening

till the snow flies. Well, we all need a rest. You keep a pretty close watch on that bank."

"Yeah, except for the one time I should have been watching"–Tipton shook his head–"when that guy came out with the sack full of money."

"That bank robbery was a terrible thing in a lot of ways." Mayor Bradshaw shook his head. "Bad for the town."

"And bad for Alec Parsons. He's finished," Wilkinson stated.

"What do you mean, finished?" Ranse asked.

"Let me put it this way. Who's going to want to deal in a bank whose manager's suspected of robbing the place?"

"But that's just plain foolish!" Ranse protested.

"Maybe so," the mayor said, "but the idea's around. Bound to hurt."

"Then there's his hatred of Germans," Tipton said.

"Oh, that doesn't mean anything," Wilkinson said.

"Well, it didn't, Tom. Alec had pretty well got over it until this young German came to town. Alec's sure he's the robber. It's all started up again."

"Like what happened at the hearing on the bay."

"What hearing?"

"Where you been, Ranse?" the mayor said. "Outfit, all German money, planning to open a fifty-million-dollar tourist complex. Biggest thing in Muskoka. They'll bring planeloads of tourists direct from Germany."

"Whew! Quite an idea."

"Yeah. Well, Alec got up at the hearing and raved about it being a perfect way for them to bring fifth columnists into the country. Said that's what happened in Norway before the last war. Went crazy as a wet hen."

"Yeah, and the bank don't take kindly to his antagonizing Germans. Too many of them around."

The gentlemen shook their heads sadly.

"Seems like ever since the robbery this town's gone nuts. Almost like something evil came to town."

"I'm afraid Alec's finished, all right. Too bad. I liked him."

"Now look here–" Ranse began, but he was interrupted by Tipton.

"There goes Miss Hot Pants."

The others turned and looked out the window. Madelaine had come out of the bank and was crossing the street to the parking lot.

"Um hmmm," the mayor said. "She is something."

"Sure like to park my slippers under her bed," Tom Wilkinson added.

"Yeah." They all sighed, as old men missing their youth.

"Guess her boy friend isn't picking her up today," Tipton commented. "Usually just happens to pull up in that sports buggy of his just as she's coming out of the bank."

"That one!" the mayor snorted. "What the hell is he doing here? We don't need his kind."

"Seems to have plenty of money."

"Yeah, I hear the OPP are keeping an eye on him. Some kind of defector, they say. Port Perkins's one hell of a poor place to defect to if you ask me." Tipton was cut off by a phone ringing somewhere behind him. He turned and walked into a small room at the back of the store. He came out in a moment. "It's for you, Ranse," he said, winking again. "You'll find the phone among the junk on my desk."

Ranse went into the office and picked up the phone. "You were right," Allenby told him. "RCMP say nobody defected from that swim team or from anything else. The name of the guy who jumped ship was Swinghammer. He got clear away. They're interested in your Schmitt. Probably be someone around to talk to him." Allenby paused, then added, "I don't think he's our man, though."

"Oh? What makes you say that?"

Another pause. "A hunch, maybe." Ranse could sense when a man was being evasive. "I'd suggest you leave him to the RCMP. I'm afraid I must go into Toronto on another matter. Be back in about a week. I'll fill you in then. Good-bye."

He hung up.

Ranse had a sudden feeling of menace. Allenby's words to Josie. Asking questions around town about him. And now this. Ranse felt panic and he knew he mustn't. There was no evidence against him–absolutely none. Unless Allenby with his damned questions had found somebody, somebody who had seen something. One of those by-standers who never realize the significance of what they've seen until someone like Allenby starts asking questions.

He paid for his coffee and left. Again he walked down the street and across the bridge, his mind working like a computer. A week. He had a week.

The boarding house had a large lawn at the front and on both sides, a lawn with flower beds, hundreds of asters in bloom. A discreet sign on a veranda post said: ASTER LODGE.

A bouncy woman answered his knock. Ranse knew her. She'd lived in this big house all of her life, only turning it into a boarding house when financial conditions forced her to do so.

"Come in, Ranse," she greeted him. "So nice to see you."

"Nice to see you, too, Mabel. Mr. Schmitt? Is he in?"

"Yes, he is. I'll call him."

"No, uh, I'll just go to his room. He's expecting me. Which one is it?"

"Oh. Well, all right: the second one down the hall."

"Thank you."

Ranse went down the hall and tapped lightly on the door. He had the newspaper clipping that Parsons had given him in his hand.

A voice said, "Come in, Mrs. Simpson."

Ranse pushed open the door. The room was small with a wooden bed, covered by a homemade quilt with butter-flies on it, an easy chair and one large window facing the lawn. The curtains, Ranse noticed, matched the bed-spread.

Willie was sitting in the chair facing the window reading a magazine. He was in shorts and looked relaxed.

A half-consumed bottle of beer sat on the floor beside the chair.

"What is it?" Willie said, without looking around. The arrogant bastard.

"Mr. Swinghammer?" Ranse said.

Willie jumped from his chair and stood facing Ranse. "McGruber! What the hell?"

"Your accent is slipping, Mr. Swinghammer."

Willie got control of himself. "You are making the big mistake, *ja*."

As he had done many times in the past, Detective McGruber was playing it by ear. And now he knew the best approach. He held the clipping out to Willie.

"Here."

Willie glanced at the paper but didn't take it. He'd obviously seen it before. He laughed, but it was slightly forced. "You don't make much sense, McGruber. And you better tell me what you want before I throw you out!"

"Take it easy. I'm just checking."

"Oh, *ja*. A detective is it? I thought you had, what you say?"

"Retired?"

"*Ja*."

"Well, I have, officially. But I've been hired by the insurance company to investigate a bank robbery."

"You? *You* have? *Wunderbar!*"

Time to get tough. "You can stow the phony accent, Swinghammer. I've checked. There were no defectors from any swimming team."

"Checked?"

"With the RCMP."

Willie was thinking hard now. "Investigating a bank robbery. Aha, I see. So you think maybe this Swinghammer . . . ."

Ranse stopped him. A good detective does the talking. "I'm interested in where you were on the afternoon of the seventh of August."

"I was swimming, maybe. Or water-skiing. No, I went

to the bay to talk to the contractor about a job. *Ja.*"

Ranse pulled a notebook from his back pocket. "The contractor's name?"

"I don't remember. Look. I don't have to answer questions. And if you think you can pin *your* bank robbery on me, you're crazy!"

"Perhaps. But you'd better come up with the name of that contractor. Mind if I look around?"

"Damned right I do. Get out of here before I throw you out!"

"Just as you say. But I'll be back with a Mountie and a search warrant."

Willie stared at him with concentrated hatred. And Ranse knew that he had him. Willie Swinghammer, all right, and the last thing he wanted was to talk to a Mountie. As soon as he'd left, he knew, Willie would go roaring out of town in his Porsche, and he'd ditch that before he got very far.

Good-bye, Willie, good-bye.

CHAPTER TWENTY-ONE

It was a play. That's what it was. Ranse McGruber was in the last act of a play. And, like any good actor, he was following a script, a script that he couldn't change. Later on, he might be able to think about it and maybe change it, but now he was caught up in the concentration of the part. And he knew what the next scene would be.

He had removed his rival from the scene. Removed him by cunning and guile and just plain good police work. He knew that Willie would get the hell out of town as fast as his Porsche could take him. By now he would be out of Ranse's jurisdiction. And Allenby's. He'd solved the bank robbery and removed his rival. Not bad.

And Allenby? Damn Allenby! A complication if there ever was one. What had Allenby meant when he told Josie that she could depend on him, no matter what? And his attitude on the phone. Something had to be done and done fast.

Then there was Madelaine. How much did she know? How much would she tell? What if Willie the criminal should panic and maybe kill her? Crazy thoughts.

Ranse McGruber, actor, almost good enough to make it in the big time, was ready for the next scene.

Madelaine lived in a cottage on the shore of the lake. Not one of the big summer places, but a small, old-fashioned cottage. There were three of them in a row and they were owned by somebody in the States who had bought them a long time ago, when land along the shore had been relatively cheap. Now the land was worth far more than all the cottages put together, and the absentee landlord was waiting until it would become even more valuable. In the meantime, he rented them for just enough to pay the taxes. They were great for people working in the summer theatre or for other transients.

Ranse drove out of town and along the lakeshore road, past ornate gates shutting off big cottages. Then, about a mile out, he branched off on a rutted sandy trail that wound between rocks and trees. About half a mile farther on, it branched off again to the end cottage, which sat on a large flat bare rock.

Madelaine's blue Datsun was parked beside it. The oaks and maples and pines were so thick that the other cottages couldn't be seen. A nice secluded spot.

Detective McGruber got out of his car and checked the ground. The big flat rock revealed no sign of his tire tracks. The sandy ruts, he knew, wouldn't hold a tread and, besides, cars going to and from the other cottages would obliterate his marks. The actors and staff of the summer theatre had all gone away.

The cottage had that mildewed, run-down look about it, with only the door and one small window on his side. All the other windows, he knew, would be on the lake side. Ranse walked towards the back door, his moccasins making no sound on the rock.

He climbed the rickety steps and knocked lightly on the door. A voice from somewhere inside shouted, "Come in, darling. It's not locked."

Ranse pushed the door open and entered. He was in a small living room, cottage-style: rattan furniture, cheap lamp with garish shade, carpet with paths made by many transient tenants, sliding glass doors leading to a full-length screened porch that faced the lake, Franklin stove for cool nights, kitchen at one side of the room, two doors at the other, which led to bedroom and bath.

Through one of these doors Madelaine came. She was stark naked, fresh from the shower, with a towel wrapped around her long black tresses and a happy smile of welcome on her face.

Ranse stared, and whatever thoughts he might have had in his head all turned to something else. Lust? Love? Veneration, even?

The smile left Madelaine's face, replaced by surprise, anger and just a bit of terror.

"You!"

An old line from a Fred Allen radio show popped into Ranse's head: "You were expecting maybe Mayor Laguardel?" But he didn't use it. He only stared.

Madelaine was the first to regain composure. "Well, this is an unexpected pleasure. Excuse me a moment, please." She turned and went back into the other room.

Ranse wanted to run after her, but he didn't. He just stood in the middle of the room. When she came back she wore a long purple dressing gown, which covered the bronzed skin but didn't camouflage the curves.

"Well." She went to the rattan couch with its faded cushions and sat down, took a pack of cigarettes from a homemade pine table beside it and lit one. "I wasn't expecting you."

"But you were expecting someone."

"Yes."

"He won't be coming."

"What? How do you know?"

"I just left him half an hour ago. By now he is many miles away."

"Please, you're not making any sense."

"Madelaine, how much do you know about Willie?"

"Well, you know. What he told you that day. He's a defector."

"No."

"You've been playing detective?"

"Not playing. I've been hired to find the robber of the bank."

"You? You have been hired to find . . . . My God!" She began to laugh, almost hysterically.

"By the insurance company."

She stopped laughing and looked at him for a couple of seconds. "And you think Willie . . . . You scared him away with that?"

"Madelaine, his name isn't Willie Schmitt. It's Swing-hammer. He's probably never even seen East Germany. He escaped from a drug seizure off the coast of Nova Scotia. Swam ashore. Maybe brought a waterproof packet with him, which would account for his having some cash."

Madelaine's composure left her. She butted out her cigarette. "Damn, damn, damn, damn! Nothing I ever do turns out any good!" She began to cry.

Ranse moved across the room and sat beside her on the rickety couch. The nearness of her almost drove him crazy. "Did you love him very much?"

"Oh, I don't know, Ranse," she answered, like a daughter talking to a strong father. "He was fun, exciting-you know."

"Young?"

"Oh, that doesn't matter. You know that. Young is strong, but young can be hard and mean." She sighed wearily. "I've got to get out of here."

"You mean away from Port Perkins?"

"Yes. They suspect *I* had something to do with that crazy robbery." She looked directly at him. "It *was* crazy, you know, Ranse. And now with Willie-or whatever his name was-a suspect."

"Where will you go?"

"Toronto, probably. I'll ask for a transfer. Alec will see that I get it. He'll have to."

Suddenly Ranse knew how it should all end, this crazy play. He put his arm around her, and her robe accidentally slipped down off her breast. He pulled her to him.

Later, as they lay on her narrow bed, she took his hand in hers.

"That was even better than the first time," she whispered.

Ranse didn't answer. He felt twenty years younger.

Her fingers crawled up his chest and into his beard. "It feels different this time."

Suddenly he came wide awake. "Different? How different?"

"I don't know, just different."

"Maybe it's because you were just a wee bit tiddly the other time."

She got up on one elbow and leaned over him, firm breasts just brushing his chest. "Oh, you think so, do you, Mr. Ranse?" She was about to say more, he knew, but she didn't. Instead, she kissed him softly on the lips. "Anyway, I like the feel of it now."

Ranse felt like a bridegroom. His heart was pounding, his muscles stiffening. He made love to her again.

Afterwards, as he lay on his back and she slept quietly beside him, he marvelled at this miracle. A second chance. Sixty-one years old and he was acting like a thirty-year-old. How long could he keep it up? Maybe five years, maybe two, maybe one. But it was worth it. What else was there in life but making love? Where had she come from, and why to him? It was a miracle.

He got off the bed, went into her little bathroom and showered. When he came out, she was sitting up.

"You are a beautiful man," she said.

He laughed. "For the shape I'm in."

"Oh, I don't mean just to look at. You are kind and gentle. A beautiful man. I think maybe I love you very much."

Blood was pounding in his ears. His chest ached with the thrust of his heart muscles. "Enough to go away with me?"

"Away? Where?"

"Away from here. Maybe to Antigua. I know a beach where the sun shines all the time. And the sand is white and the ocean blue and the rum punches are great."

"What would we do?"

"Swim. And lie in the sun, but not too long at a time: the sun can burn you to a crisp in minutes. And sail and dive for pearls and dance in the tropical moonlight."

"And make love?"

"Constantly."

"Live like the rich people? I've always wanted to do that. But all of this would cost a lot of money."

"I have a lot of money."

She said nothing to that. Just looked at him from the corner of her eye and smiled. Then, "What about your wife and your family?"

What about them indeed? Ranse shut his mind to that. They would survive without him. His marriage wasn't any good any more–not in the way that counted. He had to take this last chance.

"When?" she asked.

"As soon as we can get away." His mind was clicking like a computer. "Don't burn any bridges. Ask the bank for a leave of absence, or resign. Then we'll drive to Toronto, and in six hours, we'll be in Antigua. No problem getting accommodation at this time of year. I have a number there to call."

She rolled over and raised her arms to him. "Tomorrow?"

"No. There's a little problem I have to solve. But I'll get onto it right away. In the meantime we must be careful. Say nothing, do nothing." He pulled on his underwear and slacks, all business.

"Don't leave me."

"Got to. Things to be done. Plans to make." He leaned over and kissed her. "Remember. Say nothing. Do nothing. I'll be in touch."

CHAPTER TWENTY-TWO

On Highway 400, cruising along in his station wagon just north of the city of Barrie, Zeke was cursing the traffic. "Look at that maniac!" he raved, at a car that had passed him going at least 120 km/h.

"Why don't you pass him?" Patrick said from the back. "You could do it easy!"

"Easily," his mother corrected.

"Why don't I pass him? Because this isn't a race we're in. See those signs on the side of the road? What do they say?"

"Maximum 80 km/h. I know, but that's only fifty miles an hour! Nobody drives fifty."

"I do," Zeke told him.

"Why, Dad?" Tim wanted to know.

"Because it's the law. And good citizens obey the law."

"It's the slow drivers who really cause the accidents," Patrick informed him.

"Now who in hell told you that?"

"Don't swear, dear," Susie warned.

"Grampa Ranse told us that."

"He did, eh? Well, I hate to say it, but your grandfather is—"

"Zeke!" his wife threatened.

"Okay, okay. But he's wrong, even if he is your grandfather. Those speed limits are carefully computed so as to . . . ."

"Ranse says computers are a bunch of–"

"Patrick!" Susie stopped him before he could report accurately on Ranse's view of computers.

"Why don't you kids enjoy the scenery and stop bugging me?" Zeke advised.

"Can we climb in the back and check our equipment?"

"What equipment?"

"You know, Dad. Our snake-catching equipment."

"What do you want to catch snakes for?"

"It's their project at school. Mr. Smithers, their teacher, is a real naturalist, and they've been studying the snakes of Ontario."

"Oh."

"And Ranse said he'd take us over to Rattlesnake Island."

"Rattlesnakes!"

"Cool it, you mutt," Timothy whispered to his brother. "There's no danger, Dad. We've got leggings and all that stuff."

"And the massasauga rattler is really a timid snake. Wouldn't attack unless you stepped on him or something."

"And Ranse says there probably aren't any rattlers on the island, anyway. But we'd just as soon catch a hognose. And there are lots of them."

Zeke didn't answer. Just at that moment a Buick, travelling at least 120 km/h, cut in on him. It was closely followed by an OPP car that pulled it over onto the shoulder.

"That's what I like to see!" Zeke gloated, as they went past the two cars. "Hope they throw the book at that nut!"

"I think you'd better go with them to the island," Susie suggested, in a low voice that the boys couldn't hear from the back.

"Okay, whatever's fair."

"And please don't concern yourself with that stupid bank robbery this time."

"Okay, okay. Any other instructions?"

She patted his knee affectionately. "Not just now. Maybe later."

As Ranse paddled into the cove on the other side of Blueberry Point, he scared up a great blue heron that flapped ponderously over his head and around the end of the point. But Ranse didn't even notice. His mind was preoccupied with plans for his future. Taking off or running away or whatever one wanted to call it, he'd discovered, is no simple matter. Fortunately, everything he owned was jointly owned by Josie–the house, car, boats, everything. The bank account was a joint one, and all the guaranteed savings certificates were made out in both their names. He would leave all that to her, taking only the fortune that lay buried on Rattlesnake Island.

From a phone booth in Deepford he had called Air Canada and made reservations for two to Antigua for Wednesday, September 19. They would drive to the airport, park the car in the big indoor garage. Then he would post a note to Zeke, enclosing the key and claim ticket. He would explain in the note that he was leaving for good and going to Florida. But Florida is a big state, and there would be no way of finding him. The hardest part would be the letter to Josie. And after she received it, he knew, she would make no attempt to find him. Josie had too much pride for that.

All of this had been comparatively easy, requiring only foresight and planning. The big problem, which was not easy, was how to get the money from the island and take it to Antigua. That would require a lot of luck.

But Ranse had a plan. Getting the money out of the country was no problem. Simply pack it in a suitcase and let the airline take care of its transportation. At Antigua customs, he remembered, the officers opened some cases and allowed others to pass unopened. There was a fifty-fifty chance of his money suitcase going through unopened.

To increase the odds in his favour, he planned to use an

old suitcase he'd bought in London to bring back two tweed jackets that he'd bought there. It was a big, rectangular case made of brown cardboard-composition material, very tough and very light. The lining was a tough paper that looked something like wallpaper. Ranse planned to reline it, leaving two inches below the lining in the bottom, under which he would place the layers of bills. Into the case he would pack shirts, a jacket, and a dressing gown. As he recalled, the customs men had made a cursory examination, lifting up the corners of clothing looking for smuggled drugs or jewellery. There was again a fifty-fifty chance that, even if they did open the suitcase, they wouldn't discover the money. And if they did, surely it was no crime to bring money into a country. The suitcase was in the boathouse now, waiting for the money.

Fortunately, his passport was up to date and so was Madelaine's. No one had asked for passports when he was there with Josie, but maybe now they would require them. He had already told Josie that he had to go to Toronto on Wednesday morning on business. And, curiously, she hadn't enquired about the exact nature of the business. He would mail her a letter from the airport.

Tuesday night he would paddle to the island and get the box from the cave in the juniper patch, put the money in a sack, and replace the box. Then he would pack the money in the suitcase, ready for the next morning. There were no holes in the plan that he could see.

He turned the canoe and, avoiding the rock he knew was there, paddled towards the mouth of the cove. So, this would be his last canoeing on this lake, except for the paddle to the island for the money. He would leave it and never return. Why? he wondered.

Well, it was better to be doing something. Even if what you were doing was absurd. The world was absurd anyway. You must be doing something–planning, taking chances, pitting your brains against somebody else's brains. Striving. Striving always for gain. There was one other thing worth living for–enjoyment. Enjoyment and striving. There was nothing else.

As the nose of the canoe poked around the last point, he could see his dock and he could see two small figures standing on it waving frantically at him. His grandsons. Where did they fit into this great plan of his? Well, he preferred not to think of that, or of his other offspring and what they would think of him. This was another matter altogether, and not to be thought of.

As he paddled closer to the dock, he could hear what the kids were shouting.

"Hey, Ranse. We're ready to go!"

"We've got all our stuff, just like you said!"

"Our teacher says we can bring them to school and show the other kids."

What the hell were they talking about? Go? Go where? This was always happening to him. He was always committing himself to some project with the kids, and then forgetting all about it.

He pulled the canoe up beside the dock and Timothy reached down and grabbed the bow and pulled it over. Ranse sat looking at his grandsons, taking a good look because, he knew, this might be the last time he would ever see them.

"Are we going to take the canoe?" Patrick wanted to know.

"No, stupid! It's not big enough," his brother told him. "Everybody's coming, or just about."

"Oh, sure," Patrick agreed. "Look, Ranse, we've got the forked sticks. Dad cut them for us, and the stick with the noose on the end and the bag. Do you think we might catch a massasauga?"

Ranse remembered then. Snakes. He'd promised the boys he'd take them to the island to look for rattlers. Well, a promise was a promise, and he had the time for it. But not Rattlesnake Island. Somewhere else.

But when he got up to the house, he soon discovered that he would have nothing to say about it. His wife and daughter were busy with wieners and hamburgers and buns, and putting lemonade and ice cubes into the big thermos.

"I picked up a lump of ice for the cooler and a dozen beer," Zeke informed him. He was wearing a T-shirt and a pair of leather shorts. His black hair had been cut at just the exact length over his ears and around the back and his Larry Csonka mustache trimmed just right so that he looked exactly like every beer advertisement you ever saw.

"A picnic, eh?" Ranse was having a little trouble pulling himself back from his new and exciting future and into the mundane present. "Nice day for it, anyway."

"Maybe the last nice day we'll have. Would you hand me the mayonnaise out of the fridge, dear?"

Ranse found the mayonnaise. "Where are you planning to have this picnic?" he asked. "Nice place on Blueberry Point."

"Oh, no," Susie corrected him. "All week I've been hearing nothing but Rattlesnake Island. Dad, are there really rattlesnakes over there?"

"Well, I've never seen a live one this far east of Georgian Bay, but the island must have got its name from something. Are you afraid of snakes?"

"You know I'm not. You brought us up not to be afraid of anything. I must admit I have trouble with some of my friends, though."

"Has anybody ever been bitten by one in Muskoka?" Zeke asked.

"Not many people, for sure. Couple of years ago or more there was a girl from the U.S. who stepped on one by accident and it bit her. They took her to the doctor in Deepford, but he wouldn't give the anti-venom injection because he said he wasn't sure it had been a rattler."

"What happened?"

"I think they drove her into Toronto, but by that time it was too late."

"Did she die?"

"Can't remember exactly. Maybe we shouldn't take any chances."

"We'll be careful," Zeke assured him.

"Yeah. I guess if we stay close to the beach, where that big old stone fireplace is, we'll be okay."

"Imagine it still being there," Susie exclaimed. "You know, Zeke, this has always been our favourite picnic spot. Don't know who built it, but it must have been a long time ago."

Ranse went down to the shore, where the kids were fooling around with the canoe, and got the motorboat out of the boathouse, put in the required number of life jackets, checked the gas tanks and pulled the boat alongside the dock.

"A family picnic!" he muttered. "Just exactly what I don't need!"

CHAPTER TWENTY-THREE

As soon as the boat touched shore on Rattlesnake Island, the twins leaped off the bow and, clutching their equipment, ran into the woods. They'd been sitting on the bow peering out, like a couple of figureheads, as the island got bigger and bigger in front of them. Theirs was a singleness of purpose rarely seen except in ten-year-olds. Before the adults could move, they were gone.

"Well, that's a switch," Zeke said. "They didn't even want to eat first."

"Is it safe, Dad?"

"Yeah, mostly," Ranse assured her. "But we'll go and find them."

He and Zeke pulled the boat up on the shore and helped the women unload the food. Ranse was uneasy. He knew from experience the uncanny ability of kids to find things. No matter where he hid his fishing pole or his walking stick or his electric drill, it was no time before they located it. He could hear the boys off in the bush, shouting excitedly. He called to them, but they didn't answer.

"Come on," he said to Zeke. "There's a bit of a path through here." He led the way along an overgrown path through thick hemlock and white pine. The path ran parallel to the shore for about two hundred feet and then ended against the sheer cliff that faced the clear, deep water of the lake.

There they found the boys, peering upwards.

"How can we get up on that rock?" Timothy asked. "Our teacher says that this time of year snakes like to sun themselves on ledges."

"I bet we could climb it," Patrick said.

"Not a chance," their father warned. "Straight granite for forty feet, with no footholds."

The two boys stood holding their complicated snake-catching equipment, foreheads creased with thought.

"How about around the other side of the island?" Timothy asked.

"Sheer rock. That's why nobody has ever built on this island, why they left it for picnickers. It's really just a great big rock, with this narrow crescent along this shore."

"Hasn't anyone ever been up top?"

"Probably. But not that I know of."

"With a helicopter we could do it, easy."

"Or with ladders. Maybe we could cut trees and make a ladder!"

"That would take all day and more tools than we've got. You'll just have to do your snake hunting along this shore," Zeke told them. "I'm going back and get something to eat."

"Me, too," Ranse said. The two men went back along the path, but the boys didn't follow.

"Bet they find a way to get up there," Zeke said with a certain amount of pride. "Won't give up until they do."

Ranse was afraid he was right.

They built a fire in the old stone fireplace and Ranse laid his metal grill over it.

"There you are," he said. "When that burns down a bit, it will be perfect for hamburgers and hot dogs."

The women had set up an old folding table, covered it with a cloth and were laying out the food. Josie was happy. Ever since she was a little girl she'd loved picnics. She could remember how her father would shine up the old six-cylinder McLaughlin, which had what he called "the grubstake box" bolted onto the right-side running board. They'd load it with food and set out for a picnic somewhere along the Ottawa River. Since then, every time she went on a picnic, she'd think of him and of her mother in her neat driving costume.

Soon the hamburgers and wieners were sizzling on the grill.

"Get the boys," she told Ranse. "It's just about time to eat."

Ranse shouted for the kids, but there was no answer. Then Zeke shouted even louder, and then, from somewhere far above them, came an answering call. "Hey, we're up here!"

"Up on the top?" Ranse could hardly believe it.

"There's a secret path," Patrick shouted. "About halfway along the rock wall. It's hidden behind an old hemlock, but we found it. Come on up!"

"No!" Zeke commanded. "You come down. And right now! All the food is ready."

"Aw, nuts!"

"Can we come up again after we eat?"

"It's sure neat up here. Pine trees and moss all over the rock, and, boy, is it ever warm!"

"Okay," Zeke said. "We'll go up with you after we eat."

Ranse sat on an immense fallen log and poked at his food. So it had come down to this. Beside him the boys were wolfing down their food and jabbering like jays.

"Jeez, Ranse, wait till you see it!" Patrick said. "The moss is all dry, brown, and brittle."

"But there's some green stuff growing, too. Hey, I bet we're the first people ever been up there!"

"Except the Indians. They'd know about that secret path. Maybe they went up there for, you know, ceremonies and things."

"Oh, sure. And the place is probably loaded with buried treasure," Zeke scoffed. "Places like that always are–on television."

"Maybe it was a burial ground and we can find some bones!"

"How thrilling," their mother commented. "There are more hamburgers here. Don't you boys want any more?"

"No, thanks," Patrick assured her. "Come on, let's get going!"

"I thought maybe I'd do a little fishing off that rock there." Ranse knew there wasn't much hope, but he had to try. "Great place for bass."

Usually the mere mention of bass would arouse unbounded enthusiasm in the twins, but now they couldn't care less.

"Jeez, Ranse, we can fish any time. This might be the last chance we'll get to explore that cliff!"

The last chance indeed.

"Are you coming, Dad?" Patrick shouted, as they disappeared into the woods.

"Wouldn't miss it for the world."

"Me neither," Susie said. "After all, how often do you get to see an authentic Indian burial ground?"

"Complete with buried treasure," Josie laughed. "I'm coming, too."

"You?" Ranse objected. "It might be quite a climb."

"Well, I'm quite a climber. Come on, Ranse." She took him by the hand and there was the old comradeship and affection there. How many times had they explored new places together? How often had they shared, enjoyed, loved together? That simple act of taking his hand took Ranse's mind back to it all. And how often at times like this, when they'd been alone together in the outdoors, had they just naturally and enthusiastically come together and enjoyed each other, while butterflies flitted by and birds sang? But he had no urge to do that now.

Instead, he followed the others.

With the excited shouts of the twins leading, they found their way through the woods to the hidden path.

"See?" Patrick shouted, like an archeologist who has unearthed a new find. "Nobody would ever know it was here!"

"I still can't see it," Susie said.

"Well, just look." Timothy pushed aside the long, low

branches of a hemlock whose crown had been chewed off by porcupines, and there, sure enough, was a narrow split in the cliff. It slanted up among the roots of pines that clung precariously to the rock.

Patrick was already halfway up. "Come on!" he shouted. "It's easy. Even for you, Grandma."

They all followed, with Ranse bringing up the rear. Halfway up was a ledge, covered with dried blueberry bushes and fallen debris. More roots helped them get up over this ledge to another, and finally, with a certain amount of pulling and boosting, they all reached the top.

"Oh, look at that view!" Josie exclaimed. She was flushed with excitement and exertion, and looked younger than Ranse had noticed her looking in the past two years.

It was a view indeed. Below them was the beautiful clear surface of Wigwam Lake dotted with other wooded islands.

"I can see our bay," Susie said. "Doesn't it look grand! There's more red in the maples than I thought."

Their reverie was broken by a shout. "Hey, we found one!"

"Be careful!" Josie called. There was little growth up here, and the boys were visible, standing beside a rock and looking down.

"Keep back!" Ranse shouted, running towards them. They were standing still, leaning over something on the ground.

Patrick looked up in wonderment and said, "It's dead!"

Ranse looked at where he was pointing and sure enough, there, lying on its back, was a short, fat snake.

"Gosh!" Timothy exclaimed. "Just a minute ago it was coiled up spitting at us, and shaking its tail. It's not a rattler," he said. "Is it, Ranse?"

"Nope. See, there are no buttons on its tail," Ranse explained. "Apart from that, it looks a lot like a massasauga and, believe it or not, it tries to act like one, too."

"How?"

"By shaking its tail and rearing up. This is a hognose snake. Quite common and absolutely harmless."

"Why did it die?" Patrick asked.

"Watch." Ranse took the stick Patrick was carrying and gently turned the "dead" snake over on its belly. Immediately it flipped over onto its back and lay motionless again.

"Holy cow!"

"Just pretending to be dead. This rascal is full of tricks. First, he mimics a rattler to scare you off, and then if that doesn't work he plays dead. Watch what happens when we leave him."

The group withdrew about twenty feet from the snake. Sure enough, after a few minutes the hognose came to life, rolled over on its belly and wriggled away among the stones.

"Hurry up and let's catch him!" Patrick shouted, springing forward with his crotched stick. But the snake was gone.

"Heck! Well, maybe we'll find another." They began looking among the big rocks, getting closer and closer to the juniper bushes under which Ranse had hidden the money.

Ranse tried to think of a diversion, but, before he could turn them back, Patrick shouted, "Hey, here's one!"

"Does he have rattles on his tail?" Timothy yelled.

"Keep away from it!" Zeke shouted, and ran towards the boys with a heavy stick he'd picked up.

"He went in there!" Patrick exclaimed, pointing to the mass of juniper. "How can we get him out?"

"Was it really a rattler?" Josie asked.

Carefully, Zeke parted the juniper with his stick. There was the rock, and, sticking out from under it, the end of a tail.

"Gosh, it might be," Zeke said. "Looks like something on its tail. What about it, Ranse?"

Ranse bent over and took a close look at the tail that protruded out of a small crack beside the big rock he'd placed there.

"Can't be absolutely sure," he said, "but it looks like one."

"Oh, boy, let's get him!" Timothy yelled. "All we have to do is move that big rock."

"Gosh, a real live one!" Patrick was jumping with excitement. "Maybe if I grab him by the tail–"

"No! Don't even think of it!" Josie said. "And stand back!"

"Leave the poor thing alone," Susie added. "It's not hurting anyone."

"Normally I'd agree," Zeke said. "But this may be one of very few rattlers in Muskoka. It's up to us to kill it before there are more."

"Kill it? No!" Timothy yelled. "I want to catch it and take it to school. We can do it easily!"

"Nothing doing," his father said. "We kill it!"

Ranse stood back, observing the little tableau as he might have watched a scene on television. If they move the rock, he thought, they'll find the box. Zeke will have an idea what's in it. But there is no way anyone can tie it to me. He'll turn the box over to the police, being careful, of course, not to get his fingerprints on it. The police will return it to the bank. The kids might even collect the reward.

And the whole thing would be over. He'd be back where he was before this crazy idea took hold of him.

All he had to do was urge them to go in there after the snake, which undoubtedly had crawled into the crevice where the neat pine box was hidden.

He stood there, knowing that this was the moment of decision. He looked at his family about him, and he knew how precious they were to him. He started forward towards the group.

But Josie had taken command. "I don't think we should kill it," she said. "I most certainly don't. Even if it is the first rattler around these lakes–which I doubt–it's living up here where nobody ever comes, in this beautiful, lonely place, one of the few where Man hasn't laid his greedy hand. Why should we dig it out and bash it to pieces?''

"I just want to catch it," Timothy said.

"That's worse. Take it away from here to Toronto for a bunch of people to stare at, and keep it in a cage until it dies?''

The boys were looking very uncomfortable.

"Grandma's right," Timothy said seriously. He'd had many lectures on ecology from his teacher, and had read about conservation and seen innumerable shows on the subject on television. "Anyway, we saw it," he said. "We can tell the class that."

"To heck with that!" Patrick said. "Gosh, we came here to get a snake and there it is!"

"I say leave it alone," Susie said.

"What do you say, Ranse?" Patrick pleaded. "We could move that rock."

Ranse looked down to where the snake's tail was disappearing under the huge slab of stone. He paused, and looked out over the lake.

"I say, leave it alone."

CHAPTER TWENTY-FOUR

The sun was almost straight overhead, making it so hot that Ranse could scarcely stand to be out of the shade for more than a few minutes. He thought of the sun in Muskoka, low in the sky, shining through the bare branches, throwing long black shadows on the white snow. Muskoka was one of the few places he knew where the snow remained white all winter.

It was just past the shortest day of the year, what the radio announcers and weathermen called the beginning of winter. Beginning of winter! Hell, they'd have had winter for at least a month up there. The Grey Cup had been played. He'd listened to it on the short-wave radio, and Edmonton had won again. The Argos hadn't even made the playoffs. Well, there was always next year.

The round table at which Ranse was sitting was sheltered from the sun by an immense coconut palm. On the table beside him was a rum punch, cold and strong. The sand was as white and as clean as sand can be, and the ocean was clear and blue. Maybe this afternoon he'd go snorkeling. He'd finished his tossed salad, which he'd mixed himself at the salad bar under another tree. But he hadn't grilled a hamburger. He had to watch his weight.

But Madelaine, he knew, would want to go sailing on the barquentine riding at anchor about two hundred yards off shore, red sails shining in the sun. She had become quite the sailing enthusiast, Madelaine had, ever since their first cruise.

It hadn't been much of a cruise, really: just around to some of the islands, with the tourists play-acting as crewmen, pulling on ropes and swabbing decks and doing jobs that they'd never hire out to do. But it was all a game, with Turbo shouting the orders, and telling them to "Step lively" and "Heave to." And then they'd put ashore in Pirate's Cove, always the same cove, and have the two rum punches that were part of the deal. They didn't do much heaving-to on the return trip, being content to doze in the shade of the big red sails.

Red sails in the sunlight. What fun!

Ranse had enjoyed it somewhat the first time, although he didn't take kindly to being ordered about by that bronzed, flat-stomached, massive-chested Turbo. And he didn't care much, either, for the way Turbo put his arm around Madelaine to illustrate the proper way to grasp a rope when she was heaving-to. Anybody could see what he was up to. But women never catch on to the tricks of jokers like Turbo.

Then his mind went thousands of miles away to the shore of Wigwam Lake. Christmas holidays. They'd all be there, he knew. Josie and Zeke and the twins and Susie, and maybe even Helen and family from Regina. And Allenby. Oh, yes, he'd more than likely be there too. Ranse had no way of knowing for sure, but he had a pretty good idea. Josie was not a woman to be long without a man, and Allenby had certainly shown great interest in her. Any man would show great interest in Josie.

He could figure Allenby's thinking. The ex-British Intelligence man, of whom there were none in the world more pragmatic and devious. Undoubtedly he suspected that Ranse had robbed the bank; then, when Ranse left like that, he would be sure of it. But he had no proof. Proof would take long and careful work and planning, and there was a good chance he would never get it, supposing always that he could discover where Ranse had disappeared to.

Far better, Ranse interpreted Allenby's thinking, to let him go. It was only money, and insurance companies have lots of that. They expected to pay off. So, Ranse gets the money, and Allenby gets Josie. Allenby, he knew, would be satisfied with the bargain.

But he didn't really want to think of Allenby now. He'd always known this would be a bad day for him. But it was, after all, only one day, and like other days it would pass away and he would be all right again.

Christmas–a day for extremes of feelings. The happy it made happier; the miserable and lonely it made more miserable and lonely. Those with families enjoyed them; those without families missed them more on this day than any other. Maybe it was the only day they felt the lack.

He took a big gulp of the rum punch and let his mind wander where it would.

There was that Christmas day when the twins were about six, and Zeke had bought each a pair of skates and hockey sticks. Ranse and Zeke had worked hard all Christmas morning shovelling snow off a square of ice near the beach, had set up sticks in the snow for goals and, with an adult and a boy making up each team, had played a game of hockey.

"I'm Guy LeFleur!" Timothy had kept shouting, as he stumbled along the glassy surface on his ankles after the tuna can full of ice they were using as a puck. Then he'd trip and slide on his belly across the ice, get up again and chase the puck, with the kind of determination that makes Canadians the greatest hockey players in the world.

"I'm defence!" was Patrick's cry. Not knowing the name of any great defenceman he could emulate, he included them all in his cry, "I'm defence!"

Zeke and Ranse were on skates, too. Ranse had been skating since he was the age of the twins, and once had been a star forward for the police team. But Zeke was far better, having played semi-professional before he joined the force. Ranse envied his skill and energy. Ranse envied a lot of things about Zeke.

He wondered what Allenby would be like on skates. Probably not worth a damn.

Josie, in her youth, had been a wonder. The first place Ranse had taken her was to the old Mutual Street arena, where they had glided around the ice to the strains of "The Skater's Waltz." At the corners he would lift her clear off the ice and swing her around. He could kiss her without missing a stride.

Ranse glanced down at the new wristwatch he'd bought from a pedlar on the beach, for two hundred Canadian dollars. The pedlar, whom Ranse figured as a fence for stolen goods, said that it was worth a thousand new. But Ranse had no way of knowing. It told the day, the month, and the year, and had several other gadgets on it that he had never tried. The watch said twelve forty-five, which would be eleven forty-five at Wigwam. The place would be a mess, he knew. The kids, up early, would have ransacked the tree that stood in front of the glass doors that led to the patio. In winter these double-glazed doors were never opened, for the patio would have at least a couple of feet of snow on it already. Wrappings and ribbons and boxes and bows would completely cover the floor, wrappings that Josie had spent hours perfecting. Josie loved Christmas.

And, by now, the kids would be outside with their new sleds or skis. Zeke would have cleared a coasting path down to the lake. Allenby (Ranse was sure he'd be there) would have helped. Ranse could see them in their down-filled jackets and tuques and mitts, shovelling away, panting breaths coming from their mouths like smoke.

But mostly he could see Josie inside, cleaning up the mess and now and then testing the immense turkey. No matter how many people were coming, Josie always insisted on an immense turkey. She would be wearing all the new things she'd received–she always did that–probably a new dressing gown and a sweater and a scarf and beads. She would wear them all. When it came to Christmas presents, she was a child.

And later the men would come in and make rum toddies with dark rum and boiling water and maple syrup, always maple syrup, and nutmeg. And they'd sit with their feet up while the kids used the new slide. Or maybe Allenby would introduce them to some new English drink. What was it the Cratchits had? A bowl of steaming porter.

And from outside would come the shouts and arguments of the boys, who already would have figured out some contest with the new slide, probably to see who could go the farthest out on the lake.

Ranse shut the picture off then. He didn't want to see any more.

A motorboat had set out from the barque, skimming along over the calm, clean water. It pulled up on the white, smooth sand. Turbo and Madelaine jumped out and came running and laughing up the beach towards him.

"We're going to paint the deck black this afternoon. Turbo says black is the only colour."

She looked marvellous. All worry-lines were gone from her face, her large brown eyes squinted against the brightness. Madelaine was made for this life. And he was a lucky dog to be here with her.

The bronzed giant leaped into the empty chair beside Ranse and took a sip of his punch.

"Sure thing. Want to help us, Pops?"

Christ, I wish he wouldn't call me Pops, Ranse thought.